DATE			

SCHOOL CONTEXT AND SCHOOL CHANGE

Implications for Effective Planning

H. Dickson Corbett
Judith A. Dawson
William A. Firestone
Research for Better Schools, Inc.
Philadelphia, Pennsylvania

Foreword by Terrence Deal

Teachers College, Columbia University
New York and London

Published by Teachers College Press, 1234 Amsterdam Avenue, New York, N.Y. 10027

This publication is based upon work performed by Research for Better Schools, Inc., under a contract from the National Institute of Education, U.S. Department of Education. However, the opinions expressed herein do not necessarily reflect the position or policy of the National Institute of Education, and no official endorsement thereof shall be inferred.

Library of Congress Cataloging in Publication Data

Corbett, H. Dickson, 1950–
  School context and school change.

  "Based upon work performed by Research for Better
Schools, Inc. under a contract from the National
Institute of Education, U.S. Department of Education"—
T.p. verso.
  Bibliography: p.
  Includes index.
  1. Educational consultants—United States.
2. Education—United States—Case studies. 3. Research
for Better Schools, Inc. I. Dawson, Judith A.
II. Firestone, William A. III. Research for Better
Schools, Inc. IV. Title.
LB2799.2.C67 1984   371.2'07   84-68

ISBN 0-8077-2704-0

Manufactured in the United States of America

89 88 87 86 85 84   1 2 3 4 5 6

SS H
R

Contents

Foreword

We are now embarking on a society-wide effort to create excellent schools. It seems a worthy goal. What culture would ever aspire to mediocrity in education or permit the primary mechanism of acculturation to fall into disrepair?

Despite its present appeal, the excellence in education movement would have much more validity if it were a first. But it is not. It is part of a series of well-intended efforts to improve public education in America. Remember the excitement of creating innovative schools? How about state and federal programs to reform public schools? This was followed by school improvement efforts. Then the effective schools movement. And now the stampede toward excellence.

There is certainly nothing wrong with another initiative to improve public education. Neither is there anything pathological about the collective amnesia that disconnects this effort from its predecessors. What becomes troublesome is the tendency to forget as well lessons about how change can be encouraged—or thwarted. We did learn something from innovation in the 1960s, reform and improvement in the 1970s, and effective schools in the 1980s. To miss the opportunity to apply this older knowledge anew is to commit an unpardonable sin. It is not that clear how long the American public will support change that reinforces the status quo. Americans, like any society, draw support and excitement from rituals celebrating core values. To be American, after all, is to embrace change.

ix

And what better stage exists to dramatize these values than the public schools.

But another side of the American culture is doggedly pragmatic. We want results. The attention on excellence in education has upped the ante. Americans will want to see whether their attention and resources pay off in schools with tangible differences.

Unless we apply knowledge about what has worked (or not worked) in the past to contemporary initiatives, we will undoubtedly replicate old mistakes. With expectations running so high, it is not clear whether we can afford another expressive activity devoid of any substantive impact. Dashed expectations breed disillusionment. The higher the expectations the deeper the disappointment. Since we do know more about change in schools, it seems absolutely irresponsible not to draw upon the knowledge base now. There is too much at stake.

School Context and School Change is an important part of the literature that policymakers and practitioners need to read, for it focuses on how outside resources interplay with internal energies to bring about change. It helps to order the complexities; it highlights points where applying pressure can make a difference. Its penetrability should increase its influence.

As policymakers and practitioners read what follows, they need to compare new strategies for achieving excellence with old strategies for seeking improvements. Where are we now? Where do we want to go? How does our local strategy compare to past efforts? What resources seem most promising to help our changes stick? What key barriers can we expect, and how can these be overcome? How can outsiders play a helpful role?

In addition, readers need to consider politics and culture—dimensions of the organizations that Corbett, Dawson, and Firestone touch on in this book. What is the mix of interest groups in our situation? How can we form coalitions in support of desirable changes? How can we minimize the opposition or create arenas where bargains can be struck? Who are the key cultural players? What core values does the change reinforce or attack? How can we orchestrate the symbols of change? What kinds of occasions are needed to mourn losses and celebrate new beginnings?

Perhaps the most important contribution of this book is its identification of the interplay between outside helpers and school characteristics. In the past, we have tried too often to develop traits or recipes that all consultants or working agents ought to use. We have also assumed that schools are alike. In doing so, we have missed the important point that approaches that work in one school may not work in another. Or, for that matter, may not work in the same school under different conditions. Corbett, Dawson, and Firestone help us understand how strategies can be tailored to fit the setting.

For someone who has studied and taken part in change in schools for the past two decades, this book provides a perspective and some constant reminders of how we can engage in new efforts armed with knowledge of what has worked or flopped in preceding efforts.

Terrence Deal

Preface

Research has demonstrated that individuals external to a school greatly enhance the effectiveness of planned change projects. These "field agents" such as district curriculum coordinators, consultants, state education agency staff, and intermediate service agency staff can often be the key factors separating success from failure. Nevertheless, not all field agents and projects achieve their objectives. The same person or program can be eminently successful in one school and miserably ineffective in another.

Written primarily for those who assist schools, this book addresses the question of why change efforts work in some places and not others. Based on interviews and observations in 14 elementary, junior high, and high schools conducted over a three-year period, the basic argument is that existing school contextual conditions inevitably mingle with the change process to yield substantially different results from school to school. Indeed, the effectiveness of field agents' activities, how planning was carried out, the success of involving teachers in the process, how widely classroom changes were implemented, and how long the changes lasted were all acutely susceptible to the influence of eight contextual conditions in the schools studied. These conditions were (1) the availability of school resources, (2) the availability and nature of incentives and disincentives for innovative behavior, (3) the nature of a school's organizational linkages, (4) existing school goals and priorities, (5) the nature and extent of faculty factions and tensions, (6) turnover in key administrative and faculty positions, (7) the nature of knowledge use and current instructional and administrative practices, and (8) the legacy of prior change projects. Of course, not all conditions were influential at the same time. Some posed obstacles early in the projects and subsequently disappeared, while others did not manifest themselves until changes were actually attempted.

For field agents, all this means that each school presents its own set of challenges that must be met in ways uniquely appropriate for that school. Agents, then, must weave their understandings of school conditions into the strategies they expect to use. The product should be greater effectiveness in improving schools.

Numerous people have made critical contributions to this book. Foremost are the staffs of the 14 schools who allowed researchers to invade their buildings and infringe on scarce time. Rarely did anyone refuse to be interviewed or observed (and only then because of a busy schedule), and no one objected to the presence of outsiders. These individuals must, however, remain nameless. Equally generous with their time were field agents from the Development Division of Research for Better Schools (RBS). They provided keen insights and observations about the projects and schools. Other division staff also made important contributions to the study from time to time. The interpretations and recommendations contained herein are much the stronger as a result.

Specific individuals have critiqued all or part of the document that follows. From RBS we thank Janet Caldwell, John Connolly, Joe D'Amico, John Hopkins, Keith Kershner, Skip McCann, and Jane Roberts for their time and wisdom. Appreciation is also expressed to Michael Fullan at the Ontario Institute for Studies in Education (OISE); Michael Connelly, editor, and several reviewers for *Curriculum Inquiry*, which is also based at OISE; Terry Deal from Vanderbilt University; Karen Louis at the University of Massachusetts-Boston; and Matt Miles of the Center for Policy Research in New York. They all share credit for the book's strengths and are, of course, blameless for its weaknesses. Additional debts are owed to Mike Palladino for assistance with data management, Bruce Wilson for statistical analysis, Ullik Rouk from RBS and Susan Liddicoat from Teachers College Press for editing, and Carol Crociante and Elaine Krolikowski for typing.

SCHOOL CONTEXT
AND SCHOOL CHANGE

Implications for Effective Planning

1 Introduction

Why do some schools readily welcome new practices to improve student learning while others seem impervious to the winds of change? And why are consultants and curriculum coordinators successful in some schools and fail so miserably in the others? A decade of intensive research on school change has produced few answers to these questions. It is commonly accepted, for example, that changing urban schools is difficult. The fact remains, however, that some urban schools do change, and for the better (Benjamin, 1981). Probably no matter what kind of schools one examines, some will change constructively and others not at all. In recognition of this, researchers are beginning to turn their attention from the search for universal principles of change to understanding the conditions under which change projects succeed or fail.

This general approach was used in the study upon which this book is based. The research began as an attempt to understand how one external technical assistance agency, Research for Better Schools (RBS), could work with schools to change their instructional programs. It focused on projects initiated in a total of 14 elementary, junior high, and high schools located in a mix of rural, suburban, and urban communities. As research progressed, however, it became more and more apparent that the same people using the same techniques were having very different effects from school to school. Consequently, the research focus gradually shifted from RBS' activities to understanding how local contexts affected the relationship between change strategies and project outcomes. In other words, the purpose of the research became the identification of school conditions that affected how changes were planned, how new practices were implemented, and whether the changes lasted. The basic argument of this report is that there is an inevitable mingling of local conditions and the change process that produces different outcomes from one school to another.

To be effective, then, those who provide assistance to schools must be sensitive to these conditions and must take them into account in their work. More specifically, educational consultants, district curriculum coordinators, state education agency (SEA) staff, and intermediate service agency (ISA) personnel must systematically seek out certain information about the clients with whom they work, note differences among clients, and anticipate the potential effects on a project these differences may have. This book denotes this collection of individuals who serve schools as "field agents," and its contents are directed to this audience. The intent is to draw attention to specific school conditions that have important implications for the process and outcomes of assisting schools.

This introductory chapter provides brief background information on the study and previews later discussions about school characteristics, the change process, and change outcomes.

BACKGROUND

In 1978, RBS began to develop ways to facilitate school improvement in basic skills, career preparation, and citizen education. The final product in each content area was to be a set of procedures and materials that RBS staff or other individuals who assist schools could use to help schools identify and overcome their programmatic weaknesses. To aid the development of these new efforts, RBS entered into a cooperative agreement with 13 schools (later, one more was added). RBS worked with the schools in systematically collecting data to select project goals. The schools then determined specific changes they wanted to make and spearheaded their development. Although the innovations varied from school to school, the bulk of them consisted of alterations in instructional methods, scheduling practices, administrative behavior, or special courses and activities for students.

A CONCEPTUAL APPROACH TO PLANNED CHANGE

Figure 1 summarizes the overall conceptual approach that guided the study. The expectation was that change implementation and continuation outcomes would be products of the interaction between local school conditions and the change process—an understudied hypothesis, but certainly common-sensical. The key was to understand *which local conditions* were important, *what aspects* of the change process were particularly susceptible to their influence, and *how* all this affected project results.

FIGURE 1. Conceptual Approach of the Study

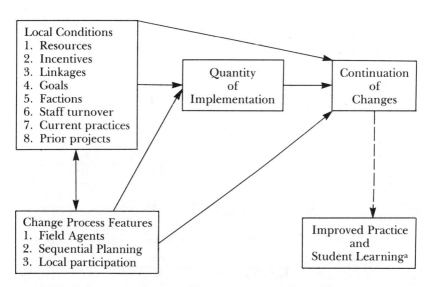

[a]Expected but unexamined relationship. Studies of school change attempt to explain implementation and/or continuation outcomes, whereas studies of school improvement seek to discover whether the changes actually prove to be beneficial. This study is of school change; one to two years provided too short a time span to make global assessments of benefit.

Figure 1 shows the local conditions, features of the change process, and change outcomes examined. Local conditions drew particular attention as the research proceeded because of the special importance that school-level factors had as influences on the change process. These factors include both organizational ones such as school resources and goals, and cultural ones as reflected in the kinds of incentives provided, staff factions and tensions, and perceptions about prior projects. Conspicuous by its absence is one often-noted influence on change—the school's environment. Issues like school-SEA relationships receive mention here but were not among the most salient factors for explaining what happened during the RBS projects. Additionally, local community concerns did not present a major obstacle, possibly because project-related changes affected day-to-day practice more than district-wide policies. To be sure, community wants and desires were always in the forefront of participants' minds; however, participants rarely pointed to them as critical issues to address.

The three features of the change process listed at the bottom left-hand corner of Figure 1 are those that were integral to the RBS change approaches, have received considerable attention in the published literature, and, most important, directly pertain to the daily work of field agents. To be a field agent means that one is physically present in schools a great deal of the time. This presence is vital to the success of change projects because agents are able to adapt, adjust, and drop procedures and materials as needed (Louis, 1981). Field agents also tend to have longer-term working relationships with a school than simply racing in to give a single workshop. Thus, the issues of sequential planning and encouraging local participation are highly relevant features of the change process as well.

Local conditions, the change process features, and the interaction between the two categories combine to influence implementation and continuation. Implementation refers to the amount of change that is initially put into place; continuation refers to the amount of change that lasts. Of course, the ultimate concern of school participants is: Do the changes that last make a difference for student learning? This question about the effectiveness of the changes is beyond the scope of this study simply because enough time had not elapsed by the study's end to assess well whether new practices had beneficial effects; the critical phenomena attended to here are whether change occurs and whether it lasts. The reader should bear in mind, however, that all changes are not worthwhile. This book is intended for use by those who have already addressed seriously the issue of the appropriateness of a proposed innovation.

The remainder of this section goes into a little more detail about local conditions, features of the change process, and outcomes. It provides a brief venture into the voluminous literature on planned change and foreshadows the major findings of the study.

Local Conditions

In school change efforts, local conditions belong to a class of events referred to by Hall, Zigarmi, and Hord (1979, p. 16) as "unsponsored interventions." That is, they are "not intended to influence use of the innovation, although, in fact, they do." The same authors point out that when such intrusions repeat themselves over time, they can be called "themes." That is the light in which one should view the local conditions presented in this book. They are themes that frequently force themselves into the spotlight, occasionally echo hauntingly in the background, and disappear, only to return suddenly to the forefront depending upon the aspect of the change process or change outcome being examined.

These conditions are likely to affect any school change project. They are already present in a school when a particular project begins (although they certainly can be subsequently altered). Eight local school conditions helped shape the change process and outcomes at the 14 schools studied. They are discussed in the order of the magnitude of their effects on the projects. The conditions are (1) the availability of school resources; (2) the availability and nature of incentives and disincentives for innovative behavior; (3) the nature of a school's linkages; (4) existing school goals and priorities; (5) the nature and extent of faculty factions and tensions; (6) turnover in key administrative and faculty positions; (7) the nature of knowl-

edge use and current instructional and administrative practices; and (8) the prior history of change projects.

More than any other local condition, the availability of
school resources influences how strategies are enacted in a
school. If staff time and the money to purchase staff time and
materials are scarce, it is unlikely that change activities will
make much, if any, headway. The source of resources is also
critical. External support for change helps initiate a project,
but it is only when a school contributes the major portion of
the resources that lasting change ensues (Berman and
McLaughlin, 1976; Chabotar, Louis, and Sjogren, 1981). Additionally, how resources such as staff time to plan an innovation
are obtained can have unintended consequences that later
make themselves felt in the change process.

Second, Lortie (1975) argues that there are very few rewards available to teachers, and the ones that are available offer
little material advantage. Nevertheless, incentives (any source
of gratification or deprivation) play a critical part in the change
process (Sieber, 1981). For example, one school may offer
money, extra planning time, or inservice credit to reward
innovative behavior; another school may only give poor evaluations for the lack of such behavior; and still another may adjust
classroom responsibilities to relieve staff of the extra burdens
imposed by participating in a project. Probably in any single
school it will be necessary to do all of the above. How the issue
is resolved has considerable implications for the success of a
change effort.

Third, research on how organizational characteristics affect
change covers a host of factors, including size and complexity
(Baldridge and Burnham, 1975; Corwin, 1975) and funding
patterns and spacial arrangements (Deal, Meyer, and Scott,
1975). This book focuses on an aspect of school organization
that more closely touches the day-to-day operation of a school
than the above factors: linkages, or the interdependence of
individuals and subunits (e.g., grade-level teams or departments). Discussions of this issue in education abound, especially
in recent literature on loose-coupling (e.g., Glatthorn, 1981;
Weick, 1982). However, concern with how work activities and
organizational members are bound to one another has a long
historical tradition in the study of organizations (Corwin,

1981). There may be a direct correspondence in some schools between change activities and subsequent behavior in the school as a whole. But given that most are loosely coupled (Miles, 1981), it is more than likely that special efforts will have to be undertaken to integrate change into a school.

The fourth local condition is school and district priorities. The better the fit between the objectives of a change project and a school, the greater the likelihood that change will result; and the more similar the change objectives are to a district's goals, the better the chance that changes will be continued (Berman and McLaughlin, 1976). When there is such a match, there is little disruption in the flow of change activities. The problem arises when change objectives fall below a district's top three or four priorities. Then, events such as a sudden shortage of resources are much more apt to interrupt the change process and require that it be adjusted before a project can continue.

Fifth, schools can be viewed from a political perspective. In this light the often-competing interests of different factions within a faculty become apparent (Firestone, 1980). Differences between teachers and administrators are obvious foci for investigation; but teachers do not comprise a homogeneous body of interests in a school. Rather, a faculty often presents a rich array of formal and informal coalitions of varying intensity and endurance. If not taken into account, such factors can sidetrack, stall, or stop the change process.

Sixth, schools vary in the amount of staff turnover. It is perhaps not too common to encounter one where a teacher with the lowest seniority in a department may, in fact, have taught in the building for 12 years. Likewise it may be equally uncommon to find a school where the coming and going of staff is so frequent that names are unknown and faces only vaguely familiar. Nevertheless, staff turnover can vary widely between these two extremes. The consequences of turnover on change projects can be considerable, especially if a principal who supports a project leaves and is replaced by another whose priorities are different. Similarly, the departure of a respected teacher who strongly advocates a project may dampen enthusiasm for it among the remaining teachers (Fullan, 1982).

Seventh, from all indications, a project has to carefully

strike a balance in how much an innovation requires behavior to depart from existing practices. Research suggests that complex efforts that seek wide-ranging effects have a high impact (Louis, Rosenblum, and Molitor, 1981); however, if projects are too ambitious they may fail (Berman and McLaughlin, 1976). On the other hand, Paul (1977) notes that the greater the compatibility of change to current practice, the greater the trivialness of the changes. The procedures used to devise an innovation can also require school staff to behave in unaccustomed ways. For example, many projects attempt to encourage the use of research-based knowledge to make decisions; yet school personnel rarely seek this type of knowledge in their day-to-day work (Hood and Blackwell, 1976). Thus, the congruence between an innovation and its associated activities with current practices in a school has considerable implications for the change process.

Finally, although Fullan (1981) indicates that there has been little investigation of the carryover effects from one change initiative in a school to another, the research literature hints that this can have an impact (Kozuch, 1979; Paul, 1977). The cumulative residue of prior projects in a school creates a legacy of change. This legacy partially sets a staff's expectations for subsequent school improvement efforts and can affect their willingness and ability to participate.

For the most part, research examines the above factors with respect to how changes are adopted rather than in a configuration also involving the change process. This book acknowledges that school context can have direct effects on change outcomes. However, local conditions also have a substantial impact on the process of change, and it is this impact that primarily influences how change activities proceed and the results they produce.

Features of the Change Process

Three of the features of the RBS change projects have been part of many change efforts and, so, have been documented amply in the literature on planned change. These are (1) the use of external field agents, (2) sequential and systematic planning, and (3) encouraging teacher participation.

Each of Chapters 3 through 5 examines the interplay between local school conditions and one of these features. Chapter 3 focuses on the use of field agents to facilitate change. A
field agent "is an individual . . . located outside of the boundaries of the client system, whose objective is to assist client(s) . . .
to enhance the clients' functioning as educators or as an educational system" (Louis, 1981, p. 180). Field agents have been
pivotal actors in educational change efforts such as the Research and Development Utilization project (Louis and Kell,
1981), the National Diffusion Network (Emrick, Peterson, and
Agarawala-Rogers, 1977), and the projects represented in the
study of Dissemination Efforts Supporting School Improvement (Crandall, Bouchner, Loucks, and Schmidt, 1982). They
have played an important part in change activities in areas
other than education as well, most notably in agriculture (Ryan
and Gross, 1943). In the 1960s and early 1970s, school improvement was dominated by an emphasis on curriculum development. Resources were poured into the creation of exem-
plary learning materials to be adopted by schools. Because
school personnel were to use the materials as designed, change
projects tended to ignore implementation issues. When it became apparent that these projects were not meeting expectations, the issue of implementation came to the forefront. Not
surprisingly, it was found that implementation was a complex
process. There were many vagaries and opportunities for
implementation to become sidetracked. Thus, school improvement efforts began to rely more heavily on field agents who
could work directly with schools to facilitate understanding of
the innovations and assist implementation activities.

Chapter 3 suggests that how the RBS field agents actually
carried out their activities at a site was very susceptible to the
influence of local conditions, particularly the availability of staff
time to plan, existing tensions and factions within a faculty, and
staff turnover. Essentially, field agents had to be flexible about
what they considered appropriate activities at a site. The ability
to adapt on the spot and to fill leadership gaps proved propi-
tious for keeping projects moving and alive.

A second change process feature (examined in Chapter 4) is
sequential, or systematic, planning. This kind of planning is

intended to lead to a school's adoption of a change that is highly appropriate for its immediate circumstances. Generally, such planning uses a problem-solving approach that involves identifying a problem, systematically collecting data on the nature of the problem, searching for alternative solutions, and selecting a solution (Hage and Aiken, 1970). The basic assumption behind such planning, of course, is that the more appropriate a solution is for a school, the more likely it is to be implemented successfully and to have beneficial results. Variants of this style of planning are provided for in the plans of most change projects (e.g., Herriott and Gross, 1979).

The question of whether highly systematic planning is possible in schools has been debated (Clark, 1981). In this study, efforts to simply conduct planning activities in a logical sequence ran into difficulty. Schools had trouble coordinating release time for teachers and buffering themselves against unanticipated demands and periodic changes in priorities. The consequence was that activities did not always occur when intended, if they occurred at all. Moreover, teachers typically based their classroom decisions on what their common sense knowledge told them. The availability of systematically collected data did not automatically change their style of decision making.

Chapter 5 addresses a feature of the change process that has received much attention in the organizational development literature: encouraging staff participation in implementation planning. This feature has assumed a prominent place in many school improvement efforts (Giacquinta, 1973). Studies conducted by the Rand Corporation showed that in schools where a process of "mutual adaptation" of the innovation occurred, there was greater likelihood that changes would be implemented and eventually incorporated (Berman and McLaughlin, 1976; McLaughlin, 1976). By providing the opportunity for participants to discuss and plan changes, greater commitment to, or "ownership" of, the innovation should ensue—along with a higher quality innovation (Bartunek and Keys, 1979). In turn, such conditions should lead to successful implementation.

In this study, participation was not always a positive influence. When teachers felt their students suffered under the tutelage of substitutes or when teachers had to forego too many planning periods, participation became a disincentive to change rather than an incentive. Thus, field agents found it necessary to occasionally reduce participation in order to maintain staff commitment to a project.

Change Outcomes: Implementation and Continuation

When is an innovation implemented? Does ritualistic adherence to an innovation's original guidelines represent more or less implementation than adapting those guidelines to unique circumstances? What are the side effects of change projects? How important are affective outcomes as opposed to technical outcomes? How long do changes last once they are made?

Studying innovation outcomes has become considerably more complex than it was in the days when the major concern was whether or not a farmer used a new kind of seed. In part, the complexity stems from moving the object of study from individual adopters—farmers—to organizations—schools (Baldridge and Deal, 1975). Another source of complexity lies in the variety of potential outcomes. For example, Larsen and Werner (1981) identify seven types of knowledge use from "nothing done" to "steps toward implementation taken" to "adaptation of information." Hall and Loucks (1977) have developed a similar but more elaborate classification of levels of use of an innovation. And these two efforts capture only the possible direct outcomes of an intervention. They ignore the numerous unintended ramifications a change project can have in an organization. Greater attention to a project's varied outcomes and how long they last is beneficial because it inevitably results in a better understanding of a project's impact. At the same time, it makes the research task more difficult because phenomena that require explanation seem to proliferate.

This study examines the number of individuals who actually made project-related changes (implementation) and who still used the new practices after formal project activities had ended (continuation). Changes are defined as any alterations of behavior participants and nonparticipants acknowledged as having been made as a result of the projects, whether they were initially intended or not. Many staff noted awareness changes as well; but unless awareness was translated into action, it was not considered as an actual change.

Chapter 6 focuses specifically on how organizational linkages within a school affect how widely implementation spreads. Current thinking about school organization notes that schools are not tightly structured bureaucratic institutions. Instead, they have a high degree of independence, or loose coupling, among actors and actions (Corbett, 1982a; Deal and Celloti, 1980; Firestone and Herriott, 1982; Glatthorn, 1981; Miles, 1981; Rosenblum and Louis, 1981; Weick, 1976). The same line of thinking suggests that widespread change is problematic where teachers are loosely linked to one another and to the administration. As a result, field agents face major obstacles in facilitating school-wide changes.

In this study, this notion held true. The more independent teachers were and the less congruence there was among staff about school priorities, the lower the quantity of implementation. A critical finding, however, was that no school displayed uniformly loose or tight linkages. Instead, there were considerable differences across grade levels or departments. To be effective, a field agent has to map the organization of a school by noting where interdependence and independence exist and, then, must use different strategies for spreading change to the various subunits within a school.

Chapter 7 carries the examination of change outcomes one step further. It looks at what happens to change over time. Research indicates that once changes are made, they do not automatically last. Instead special care has to be exercised to ensure that (1) changes become part of operating routines, (2) individuals making changes continue to receive encouragement and support for engaging in new practices, and (3) assessments of the effectiveness of the new practices take place (Corbett, 1982b; Glaser, 1981; Yin, Quick, Bateman, and Marks, 1978). If the above do not occur, the fruits of change efforts quickly wither.

This study affirms the above conclusions for schools. Numerous teachers described the tendency for effects of previous projects to die out rapidly once the attention of administrators and field agents turned elsewhere. In the RBS projects, unless provisions were made to maintain some level of incentives for teachers to continue new practices or to incorporate the new practices into curriculum guidelines, the new practices were discontinued before any assessments of their effectiveness could be made.

A FINAL WORD ABOUT THE AUDIENCE

This book is directed to field agents. Although Chapters 3 through 7 support explanations, interpretations, and arguments with considerable data, the data are there as much to convey the texture of school life and its interaction with the change projects as they are to persuade other researchers that the findings are accurate. Moreover, at the end of each chapter the discussion returns to the question: So what does this mean for field agents? This issue is addressed in even more detail in the concluding chapter.

Obviously a study of 14 schools will not be the ultimate and comprehensive statement on how field agents should work with schools. This work has no aspirations to be that. What it does aspire to do is (1) to identify specific ways in which local school conditions can vary and (2) to trace how these local conditions affect the change process and change outcomes. The intention is that such information will provide grist for the mill as field agents ponder how they should work with particular schools.

2 Overview of the Study

Surprises seemed to be the rule rather than the exception in all of the 14 projects studied. Just as a project appeared doomed to failure, interest in it would revive; similarly, where success seemed assured, disruptive influences would emerge. What this says is that schools are unpredictable. Familiarity with them does not protect against the unexpected. A school is a school is a school may accurately reflect the ruminations of people remembering dull adolescent days, but this attitude can quickly lead field agents astray if applied to the task of providing assistance.

Likewise, when it comes to studying schools, researchers must guard against overconfidence. Research procedures must leave room for the unexpected to hit one over the head. To enable this to happen, this study relied on unstructured and semistructured interviews and observations. The intent was not to cast away preconceptions but to inform them. This chapter introduces the projects, the schools, and the research methods. It conveys the richness and variety of the settings and explains how the research procedures attempted to capture them.

THE PROJECTS

Three organizational components within RBS' Development Division had the responsibility of designing approaches to school improvement in basic skills, career preparation, and citizen education. Each topic had been designated as a priority by state departments in RBS' service region. Although general corporate guidelines set broad parameters, each component had considerable leeway in accommodating both the state of the art in its field and the experience of its staff.

Despite differences among the three approaches, they had four characteristics in common. First, each relied on field agents to be the major contacts with the schools. The term *field agent* is simply a designation for an individual who bridges the gap between schools and sources of external information. The RBS agents shared technical information, assisted planning, and located materials to support the schools' efforts to improve. Second, the three approaches were developmental. That is, at the same time that RBS helped schools improve, it was field-testing and refining the approaches themselves. School staff consented to this two-way flow of assistance and rarely seemed troubled when told, for example, that a certain planning activity was an experiment that could possibly fail. Third, RBS was committed to involving a broad spectrum of local staff in planning activities. At a minimum, planning groups included teachers and building administrators; most also incorporated counselors and other district office staff. Fourth, schools did not pay RBS for its services. RBS covered the costs of development, field agents' time, and the necessary printed materials; in return, schools agreed to release project staff to attend meetings.

Of course, there were differences in the components' approaches. The *basic skills* projects focused on increasing students' time-on-task and clarifying overlap in students' learning, the content of reading and math instruction, and achievement test items. Teachers gathered data on their classroom operations and compared these data with research findings on what the probable learning outcomes would be. From these comparisons, teachers and administrators could pick out where instruction needed to be improved. Some of the classroom-level changes made included reducing the transition time between activities, using more whole-group instruction, resequencing instructional content, and reallocating instructional time. Occasionally, however, building-level changes were also made, for example, rescheduling art or music classes, adjusting the way special education students were pulled from regular classrooms, and revising teacher supervision practices. Five elementary schools and one middle school that participated in basic skills projects were included in this study. Of these, the middle school and two of the elementaries took part only in the project's first year; research data for this study, however, were collected at the schools for three years.

In *career preparation* RBS worked with three high schools and one junior high. The intent was to integrate the topic into other subject areas, especially math, science, English, and social studies. The assumption was that all students needed help adjusting to the world of work, not just those about to leave high school. Specific aspects of work emphasized at a school were agreed upon through a series of planning meetings, surveys, and investigations of other career programs. Once a planning committee formulated its goals, it began to develop objectives and activities to meet them. A pilot test of potential changes then followed. One major change eventually made in all four career education schools studied was the incorporation of career-related activities into regular subject courses. In addition, some schools developed special career education courses and displayed related career materials so that they would be accessible to all teachers. At the junior high, a new principal formally withdrew the school from the program after the second year, but some project-related activities continued.

The *citizen education* projects were similar to those in career preparation in that all four junior highs that participated used a systematic planning process to identify goals. Planning committees also included community representatives because both RBS and the schools expected that improved community-school relations would become one of the goals selected. Project-related changes were made in classrooms where teachers infused citizen education activities into regular courses and in the ways in which certain student behaviors were rewarded. RBS worked with the schools for a little over one year before federal support for the effort was withdrawn. Formal on-site research observations at these sites also ended at that time. However, more than a year and a half later, researchers returned to the schools to interview staff about what from the projects had survived.

The criteria used to determine which schools were selected to collaborate with RBS differed in each project area. In basic skills, schools were first nominated by intermediate service agencies; in career education, they were selected on the basis of their previous interest in obtaining special state assistance funds for career programs; and in citizen education, RBS staff sought schools that had acute social problems. The participating sites are described in more detail below.

THE SCHOOLS

The 14 schools in the study represented a diverse mixture of size, type of community served, and student body composition (Table 1). The following thumbnail sketches introduce the research sites and provide a flavor for the kinds of institutions RBS staff found once in the field. Appendix A contains addi-

TABLE 1. The 14 Schools

Name	Level	Number of Classroom Teachers	Percent of Minority Students	Community Served	RBS Project
Middleburg	Elementary	31	11%	Suburban	Basic skills
Middletown	Elementary	22	21%	Suburban	Basic skills
Patriot	Elementary	18	95%	Small city	Basic skills
Smalltown	Elementary	35	33%	Rural	Basic skills
Southend	Elementary	13	20%	Rural	Basic skills
Farmcenter	Junior high	43	19%	Small city	Citizen education
Green Hills	Junior high	45	8%	Suburban	Career preparation
Riverside	Middle	63	96%	Big city	Citizen education
Smalltown	Middle	38	21%	Rural	Basic skills
Suburban	Junior high	49	2%	Suburban	Citizen education
Urban	Junior high	77	61%	Big city	Citizen education
Bigtown	Senior high	150	92%	Small city	Career preparation
Neighbortown	Senior high	49	0%	Rural	Career preparation
Oldtown	Senior high	141	55%	Small city	Career preparation

tional descriptive information on how the projects progressed at each site. The reader may want to refer to this appendix while reading the following section. School names used throughout this report are fictitious.

Middleburg Elementary

Middleburg is located on the fringes of a major urban city and is one of the earliest suburban developments in the area. Its residents are split between those who commute to the city to their jobs and those who work in local factories. The school has 31 teachers and enrolls more than 650 K-6 students, about 90 percent of whom are white. Just before the beginning of the RBS project, declining enrollment forced the district to lay off over 100 teachers and shift some administrators back to classrooms. According to the principal, the decline had been as much as 30 percent over the previous four years. The school was one of the five original basic skills sites. However, at the beginning of the project's second year, the principal opted to allocate staff development resources to another project and so withdrew the school from further work with RBS.

Middletown Elementary

Middletown replaced Middleburg as a basic skills site. School administrators there had already observed several RBS meetings at another project school and were keenly interested in pulling up the level of students' math and reading skills. The school continued in the project for the remaining two years of the study. Middletown is in a community very similar to Middleburg's, but with a greater racial mix and a less dramatic declining enrollment. The school is about two-thirds the size of Middleburg, in terms of numbers of teachers and students, and is the only elementary school in the district.

Patriot Elementary

Patriot is a K-4 school in the heart of a medium-sized city. The school, and many of the surrounding buildings, are monuments to the typical factory style of urban architecture prevalent in the early part of this century. Eighteen classroom teachers are responsible for slightly less than 400 children, almost all of whom come from minority groups. As the project began, administrators said they were beleaguered with low achievement levels; Patriot's principal estimated that 75 percent of the students were at least a year behind in reading. Additionally, the school was informally projected by the state education agency as one of 30 schools unlikely to meet proposed minimum standards. The school participated in the basic skills project for all three years of the study.

Smalltown Elementary

In sharp contrast to Patriot, Smalltown Elementary is located on the edge of a small farming town and is surrounded by open fertile fields. The newly constructed school houses 35 classroom teachers and over 600 students in grades one through six. The school's emphasis is on providing a variety of instructional styles in an open-classroom situation. The proportion of white students to minority students is roughly two to one. The number of advanced degrees held by Smalltown's faculty is one of the two lowest of the 14 schools studied. Nevertheless, there is a considerable flow of new ideas through frequent staff development projects initiated by the superintendent. After involving the school in the basic skills project for one year, the superintendent shifted its staff development focus to another area.

Southend Elementary

Southend is in the same district as Smalltown Elementary. However, at this site, the superintendent kept Southend in the project for all three years. Unlike Smalltown's emphasis on open-classrooms, Southend's priority is attention to the basic skills of reading and math. Along with this, there is a close watch on student discipline. Strategically placed signs continually remind staff, students, and visitors to lower their voices and to move safely in the halls. Families in the community may send their children to either of the two schools. Southend is smaller than Smalltown, with 13 teachers serving less than 300 students in kindergarten through fourth grade.

Farmcenter Junior High

Farmcenter presents some interesting contrasts. To reach the medium-sized city in which it is located, a traveler passes through one of the richest, highest-yielding farm regions in the United States. The school itself, though, is in the third largest district in the study and its imposing one-building campus is squeezed into a neighborhood of inner-city-like row houses. Only slightly more than 20 percent of its 43 teachers have advanced degrees, in spite of the fact that the shadows of a sizeable university fall across the schoolyard. According to the principal, 75 percent of the nearly 700 students (80 percent of whom are white) are at least one year behind the average in reading. Farmcenter took part in the citizen education project until the project terminated shortly after its first year.

Green Hills Junior High

Green Hills is a typical suburban school. The building is relatively new and cleanly kept; its spacious playing fields are enclosed by large, colonial-style homes; and class period transitions are orderly. Completing the familiar portrait is a largely homogenous student body with a high percentage of parents who attended college. The students who have severe reading problems are so few that the principal could almost list them by name. The one major problem confronting the principal and the school's 45 teachers is declining enrollment. A recent 20 percent enrollment drop compelled the school board to look for ways to reduce staff and programs. Participation in RBS' career education program provided one way for the principal to show that efforts were being made to upgrade all instructional areas and that none should be candidates for reductions. However, the principal moved to a district office job after the project's second year and the new principal declined to accept subsequent RBS assistance.

Riverside Middle School

Riverside's appearance is the opposite of Green Hills. Barred windows, locked doors, graffiti, and an almost ever-present police patrol car are the distinguishing landmarks at this sixth-through eighth-grade school. The principal estimates that 90 percent of its nearly 1,000 students have severe difficulty reading. Because of the many learning and behavioral problems the school faces, staff have learned the ins and outs of various forms of outside assistance. The result has been that many of the 63 faculty look at such assistance askance. Although the school participated in the citizen education project until its end, the number of faculty who participated from meeting to meeting fluctuated greatly.

Smalltown Middle School

Southend and Smalltown Elementary students graduate to this rural, 6–8 school. Smalltown Middle School has 38 teachers and roughly 575 students. About one-fourth of the students lag at least one year behind in reading. The school formally participated in the basic skills project for one year, at which time the superintendent initiated other staff development opportunities for the faculty.

Suburban Junior High

Suburban is much like a composite of the other schools in this study. Like Farmcenter, it is located in a farming region. However, as is the case with three other schools, its proximity to major cities makes the area attractive to large numbers of commuters. Its school district is the second smallest in the study, behind Middletown's. Forty-nine teachers serve 830 adolescents, two percent of whom are minority students. This degree of student homogeneity is only exceeded at Neighbortown. The principal reported that enrollment had not declined at all in the four years before the beginning of the citizen education project. Only the three schools in Southend's district and Neighbortown had similar situations. As did Farmcenter and Riverside, the school remained in the citizen education project until the project ended.

Urban Junior High

Although this urban school officially remained in the citizen education project until the project's close, the effort never really got off the ground. Teachers continually questioned the wisdom of devoting resources to this kind of project when there were more pressing problems such as a lack of heat, inadequate student nutrition, and widespread reading deficiencies. Making obstacles even more difficult to overcome was the fact that the district's desegregation plan had filled the buildings, located in a nearly all-white neighborhood, with 61 percent minority students. The school's 77 teachers, over half of whom hold advanced degrees, instruct 1500 students.

Bigtown High School

Bigtown has the largest faculty of the schools in the study. The 150 teachers work with more than 2,600 students, 92 percent of whom come from minority families. The school belies its urban designation. It is surrounded by neat, well-kept residential neighborhoods, and its sprawling campus shows few signs of vandalism. Moreover, the principal estimates that less than half of the students have reading difficulties. The administration regards preparing students for the world of work as a top priority. This emphasis naturally attracted RBS to the school. Bigtown participated in the career education project for all three years.

Neighbortown High School

Neighbortown serves a rural community whose economic base is in agriculture and small industries. Its bucolic setting and proximity to major transportation routes have lured branches of several large companies as well. This apparently happy situation creates a problem at the high school: students drop out of school because employment is so easy to obtain. To a great many of the school's 800 teenagers, the prospects of earning five dollars an hour during time normally spent in the classrooms of Neighbortown's 49 teachers is too tempting. Moreover, few of their parents have continued their education at colleges and universities. Thus, school and district administrators were anxious to use RBS' career education project as a way of expanding students' conceptions of the world of work.

Oldtown High School

Upon entering Oldtown's 60 year-old building, a likely assumption might be that this high school is the urban receptacle of the graduates from Riverside or Urban. The granite block structure consumes an entire city block; 141 teachers wear identification badges so that they can be distinguished from visitors; and even when classes are in session, there seems to be constant student movement in the hallways and on the outside steps. Yet if a visitor scans the adjacent neighborhood, strains to identify background sounds, and breathes in the air, the senses correct the first impression. Oldtown is only a few blocks away from sandy beaches, the crashing surf, and a glittering array of resort businesses. Still, academic problems abound. The principal guesses that 60 percent of the more than 3,000 students have fallen at least a year behind in reading. Also, the school struggles continually to meet a steady stream of state regulations. Consequently, the school's participation throughout the three years of the RBS career education project was episodic— a mix of enthusiastic attention and lengthy inactivity.

THE RESEARCH

Data were collected primarily through qualitative research procedures, such as formal and informal interviews, informal observations, and document reviews. Information was recorded in the form of written field notes by researchers at each site. These notes comprised the data base for subsequent analysis. The research followed a comparative case study approach in that the intent was to understand planned change events in 14 sites and then identify commonalities across the sites (Yin, 1981). As was true in this study, this kind of research is often conducted without actually writing case studies on individual sites. Instead, analysis draws out cross-site comparisons. Obviously such an analytic approach precludes a detailed presentation of the change process at any one school; the trade-off is that the reader should come away with much keener insights into the change process itself.

Qualitative methods were especially appropriate in this study for three reasons. First, one of the guiding assumptions of the study was that school context would have a critical impact on how the change process was enacted and on eventual outcomes. Qualitative methods particularly facilitate fine-grained analyses of the interaction between organizational settings and individual behavior (Wilson, 1977). Second, when the study was initiated, implementation was poorly documented in the literature. Most research had focused on adoption of inovations, ignoring what happened to new practices and materials as they were actually used or discarded (Fullan and Pomfret, 1977). Repeated interviews and observations made it possible to collect data on events as they unfolded over time, thereby enabling researchers to see just where changes were made, what success was achieved, and what fates the changes eventually met. Finally, in observing events, it is important to understand the meanings participants attach to them. Often what is significant is not the reality of events as they are seen by external observers but what the perceptions of the actors involved are. Thus, project participants' viewpoints were an invaluable source of data for suggesting and corroborating interpretations of why events turned out the way they did.

In the first year, researchers examined the initiation of the change projects in all 14 schools. Also, teachers completed surveys on the organizational characteristics of their schools. A full report on these surveys is available elsewhere (Firestone and Herriott, 1981a). The surveys are used in this book only at the beginning of Chapter 6. Then, in the study's second year, intensive fieldwork in five of the schools provided richer data on the intricacies of change processes and implementation. During this time, occasional visits and interviews helped track activities at the other schools. The third year of the study was devoted largely to a series of interviews at all 14 sites to determine what happened to changes after formal project activities had ended.

Managing and analyzing qualitative data so that the full range of data can be used present major obstacles for qualitative researchers. Surprisingly, these topics are only minimally addressed in the literature on this kind of research (Miles, 1979). For this reason, Appendix B describes, in detail, the procedures used in this study to store and code data and to use data to explain events at the sites.

Although the literature does not clearly elaborate on the art of analyzing qualitative data, these methods are growing in popularity (LeCompte and Goetz, 1982; Rist, 1980; Yin, 1981). However, such research can often be time-consuming and costly, diminishing its practicality for those who work with schools. Appendix C suggests ways that may help field agents obtain qualitative data that can be useful in their work and be collected with a minimal burden on resources.

3

The Change Process: Field Agents

We were there at 9:30am and as usual, no one else was. . . . The director of the cafeteria had a heart attack so the RBS field agent had a bit of a hassle getting coffee for the meeting. The field agent did go out and buy donuts this time and got some chocolate milk for the non-coffee drinkers, but there were still some requests for tea. About 10:45am, the meeting began with the local coordinator reviewing what had happened the week before. . . . The coordinator said I don't know how many of you got copies of the goal statement. . . . At this point, I looked around and I didn't see any copies of the goal statement on the table. . . . The field agent had asked the coordinator to get copies of the goal statement made and the coordinator apparently was afraid to go into the principal's office and try to do that. So the field agent went in and tried to talk one of the secretaries into doing it.   (From the Riverside field notes)

This meeting's main presentation was to be done by the assistant principal, not by RBS. The field agent had given the assistant principal the linker's manual. . . . The assistant principal had put together the talk. . . . The meeting was scheduled to start at 3:15. . . . People milled around for a while, and about 3:15 the superintendent kind of looked around at people and said, "Dearly beloved" (drawing laughs from everyone). . . . [Later] the superintendent said the meeting went very well and the field agent agreed. A couple of people complimented the assistant principal on the assistant principal's speaking ability. (From the Smalltown Elementary field notes)

26

We arrived at about 8:30. The field agent greeted me with a disconcerted frown—three teachers [out of five on the team] were absent that day. The field agent had spent some time before the session in the faculty lounge. The field agent got the feeling that teachers were upset about something with the principal. Moreover, the janitor had mistaken the field agent for a planning team teacher's substitute and said that the teacher had left the day before saying "[I am] never coming back [to this school]." . . . The field agent wanted to hold the meeting up further [than 9:10 am] to wait for the principal who was in the office with somebody, but decided to go ahead because the field agent wasn't sure when the principal would arrive. . . . [Later, after the meeting,] the field agent suggested that the teachers are afraid to discuss things in front of the principal. The field agent went on to point out that a teacher asked a question about who would be doing the observing while the principal was outside of the room. (From the Patriot field notes)

Three field agents in three schools. All shared the same conviction that the key to successful school change was for the school to take major responsibility in directing the RBS project. Yet, their activities, as reflected in the vignettes, were widely disparate. In the first school, the agent arranged refreshments and coaxed recalcitrant support staff into providing copies of materials. In the second, the agent supplied knowledge resources and then stepped back to observe. In the last school, the field agent detected tension between teachers and the principal and began to wrestle with how to mediate it and lessen its repercussions on project activities.

Why the differences in behavior if the ultimate objective was the same? The answer is that the field agents responded to idiosyncratic features in a school's context that demanded that adjustments and substitutions be made in how to promote a school's assumption of leadership responsibilities. Thus, creating a congenial atmosphere at a meeting and ensuring the availability of necessary information were critical in keeping the change process moving smoothly enough for local leadership opportunities to arise. Anticipating the impact of conflict between the principal and teachers on the principal's ability to direct the project became a salient issue if the field agent wanted to keep the planning team together. Indeed, only in the second vignette was the field agent able to encourage school responsibility directly.

This chapter shows that some field agent activities work for some purposes in some places at some times, and what works for what purpose is mostly determined by the place and time. The chapter focuses on aspects of school context and emphasizes the flexibility that a field agent must demonstrate in approaching a site and establishing intermediate objectives for enhancing the probability of successful school change.

The first section of the chapter briefly reviews research on effective field agent behavior and offers an explanation for its ambiguous findings. The next section closely examines local school conditions and their relationship to field agent behavior. It attempts to make sense out of a very intricate mix of conditions and behaviors by highlighting patterns across the 14 sites. In the third section, school staff comment about notable aspects of field agent activities. These comments suggest that field agent efforts to adjust their behavior to conditions at a site did not go unnoticed; these efforts were, in fact, considered to be largely responsible for the field agents' effectiveness. The chapter closes with a summary of key lessons from the discussion.

A LOOK AT FIELD AGENT RESEARCH

The consensus in the research literature seems to be that the use of field agents effectively promotes school change (Louis, 1981), particularly when the changes are externally developed (Emrick, Peterson, and Agarawala-Rogers, 1977; Stearns and Norwood, 1977). Field agents seem especially useful in facilitating innovation at the school level (Loucks, 1982). However, despite many instances of effectiveness, researchers have not been able to identify many specific behaviors that consistently lead to this success.

For example, Louis (1977) and Louis and Kell (1981) found that by establishing a long-term relationship with a client, a field agent could positively influence the use of the information that the agent brought to the site. However, this finding is tempered by results from another study (Loucks, 1982) that indicated that the more time an agent devoted to training local staff, the less implementation occurred. Along the same lines, an examination of field agent behavior in the first year of the RBS projects (Firestone and Corbett, 1981) found no relationship between the development of a school's commitment to a project and the frequency of agent interaction. Similar ambiguity surrounds the effectiveness of other kinds of field agent behavior.

Qualitative data from two of the above studies point to a possible interpretation of this untenable finding (both theoretically and practically) that high field agent involvement with a site can have both positive and negative effects. Louis and Kell (1981), using case study data, concluded that one of the common characteristics of effective field agents was their ability to adapt their behavior to site conditions. During the first year of the RBS projects, agents acted as on-site adjustors, negotiating the interaction between a site and an externally developed approach to curriculum change (Firestone and Corbett, 1981). What seems to happen at a site is that field agents confront barriers to school change posed by the interaction of an innovation with idiosyncratic features of the site, such as competing time demands, administrative reluctance to assume full leadership of a project, and inability to coordinate actions and events so that they fully mesh (Charters and Pellegrin, 1973). Specific barriers and how they are best overcome can vary from site to site. Thus, what field agent behavior is effective at a particular school must be determined in light of knowledge about the school's context.

In schools such as two of those in the opening vignettes, effective behavior means developing an intense, time-consuming (almost a visit a week for a year or more) relationship with a site. This kind of relationship is necessary in order to discern the barriers confronting a project and to attempt to overcome them. At schools such as the one in the second example, intensive field agent involvement may actually constrain the development of school commitment, especially if the field agent assumes most of the project leadership responsibilities. This would effectively exclude willing, competent, *and* available staff from deep involvement and probably discourage them from expending much effort on making changes.

The data presented in the next section support the argument that effective field agents have to adjust to the nature of local conditions.

FIELD AGENTS AND LOCAL SCHOOL CONDITIONS

The field agents were the major point of contact between RBS and the schools. They were frequently in touch with the sites (typically at least five times a month in person, over the phone, or through the mail) and worked with the local planning teams at each school. The agents' technical functions were (1) to promote program improvement by bringing knowledge about successful educational practices and the change process to schools, (2) to help local staff develop the capability to direct the change process themselves, and (3) to provide feedback to RBS' development specialists on necessary revisions in the process.

In terms of existing conceptualizations of agent roles, RBS agents most closely resembled Piele's (1975) process-helper. A process-helper actively identifies a school's problems by helping to collect and analyze data, but remains neutral with respect to decisions about which problems the school addresses and about remedies to those problems. RBS hoped that leadership for all project activities would gradually be assumed by school staff because such responsibility would promote local ownership of the program. In turn, ownership would facilitate the implementation of changes and the incorporation of these changes into the daily routine once the field agents' involvement ended.

Field agents described their intentions this way:

> It may have sounded like we provide you with research on your concern. Our business is not to provide technical assistance. If you have something that we can't cover directly, we'll direct your concerns to [central office staff] and they'll get you to the right person. . . . To us research is to help you with this . . . process.   (From the Patriot field notes)

> Let's talk about roles and responsibilities. I won't be leading this session after today. I'll be working with a coordinator as a

consultant. I'll be going through the agenda with the coordinator for each step.   (From the Bigtown field notes)

Let me give you a little overview of the process. We'll be having two orientation meetings. After that second orientation meeting, I'll be fading into the background. I'm not officially a member of this team.   (From the Oldtown field notes)

How dogmatic?—you might say. Not at all. . . . At any point in the process you can decide to change you[r] goals, to change the sequence of activities, whatever—it's up to you.   (From the Farmcenter field notes)

And as the Southend superintendent echoed:

I'll give you the people working with the 12 teachers. They'll make the presentation and you will act as resource people for them. I want my people to get the "invented here" message across real strong and I want to act as if it's our program. (From the Southend field notes)

In reality, of course, such clear delineations of field agents' spheres of responsibility did not always come to pass. In fact, less than a year after the Southend superintendent issued the above statement, the principal at Southend remarked, "One cannot run an inservice and take care of everything else. What I need is for someone else to come in and do it." Thus, providing project materials, training local staff to lead the project, and offering feedback to other RBS staff were hardly enough to keep the schools moving through the change process. As indicated earlier, attending solely and directly to the goal of school change was often subordinated to more immediate concerns, such as obtaining resources and developing the social relationships necessary for the change process to continue.

The Relationship Between Context and Activities

Field agents' experiences in the 14 schools indicated that four categories of contextual conditions affected the mix of agent activities necessary to smooth over rough spots in the change process. These were (1) the availability of resources to support project activities, primarily staff time, staff knowledge of the program's content area, and clerical resources; (2) the extent of tension among staff factions; (3) the amount of staff turnover and disruptions to the schools' daily routines; and (4) staff expectations about the usefulness of external assistance, based largely on their experiences in previous projects. It should be noted here that the local condition category of staff turnover is expanded in this chapter to include other disruptions that frequent school life. Unannounced meetings and staff absenteeism did not have any permanent effects on other features of the change process or its outcomes; but when they cropped up on the day of a project meeting, they did limit the number of staff available to participate.

Although in each school field agents performed the three technical functions described above, at times some agents had to supplement these in order to respond to certain school contextual conditions. They did this by (1) expanding their process-helping activities to include leading meetings, solely establishing meeting agendas, and writing funding proposals for the school; (2) adjusting the process at a specific site apart from developmental changes that RBS made in the approaches as a whole; (3) providing clerical support like typing, duplicating, obtaining audio-visual equipment, or arranging for refreshments; (4) seeking periodic reendorsements of the project from new administrators; and (5) mediating the effects of intrastaff tensions.

Table 2 juxtaposes the four categories of local conditions with the five categories of extra field agent activities. As the table shows, agents compensated for low levels of resources by expanding process-helping (at seven schools), making idiosyncratic adjustments in the process (at seven schools), or providing clerical services (at five schools). Acute outbreaks of intrastaff tension necessitated mediating their effects on staff and the project at five sites (and, in two instances, led to adjusting the process). Two activities undertaken in responding to high levels of staff turnover and other unexpected disruptions in school life were expanding process-helping (at three schools) and seeking reendorsements (at three schools). Staff expectations for field agents posed special problems at three urban sites and were dealt with by adjusting the change process. At the other sites, staff seemed to suspend their attitudes about previous projects, adopting a more neutral posture toward field agents. In these cases, expectations did not compel new activities so much as they reinforced particular activities once RBS agents performed them.

The following four sections amplify the information in Table 2. Each section examines how field agents took a school condition (listed in the four columns) into account in trying to maintain progress in the projects.

Resource Availability

The availability of resources was the most important and continuous obstacle that field agents faced. At some point at every school field agents had to compensate for resource shortages. At 11 of the schools, shortages were frequent enough that field agents consistently moved beyond the activities required solely by the three RBS approaches.

Among the resources most needed to support project activities were staff time to plan and implement changes, staff knowledge about the program content and expertise in planning, and clerical support. Shortages of any of these resources threatened a school's ability to move through the process. When the costs of participation became too high, staff began to question whether they should continue. At these times, field agents stepped in. By expanding process-helping, adjusting the process, or providing clerical services, they reduced costs and paved the way for planning to go forward.

Time. The time of teachers, principals, and other school staff was a critical resource needed in all of the schools. But providing this resource was more problematic in some schools than in others. Most schools managed to free teachers so that they could attend meetings. (Although how this was accomplished occasionally had a ripple effect throughout the life span of the project, as will be discussed further in Chapter 5.) However, three schools had special difficulties. At Patriot and

TABLE 2.   Field Agent Activities and School Conditions at Sites

		SCHOOL CONDITIONS		
FIELD AGENT ACTIVITIES	*Availability of Resources*	*Tension Between Factions*	*Staff Turnover and Disruptions*	*Expectations from Prior Projects*[a]
Expanding process-helping	Green Hills Urban Bigtown Neighbortown Riverside Patriot Southend	Patriot	Urban Riverside Patriot	
Adjusting the process	Middletown Suburban Oldtown Bigtown Neighbortown Riverside Patriot	Patriot Suburban		Urban Bigtown Riverside
Providing clerical services	Green Hills Urban Riverside Farmcenter Patriot			
Seeking endorsements			Green Hills Middleburg Patriot	
Mediating		Green Hills Neighbortown Riverside Patriot Urban		

aExpectations influenced field agent behavior at other sites than the three listed. But in these other cases, expectations reinforced activities once they were performed. Only at the three sites did expectations initially shape field agent behavior.

Riverside, substitutes were not generally available, and when they were, teachers questioned their competence. As a result, meeting days occasionally spawned traumatic incidents over whether a substitute would show up and what would happen in a class when one did. The effect was that a field agent could never be sure of the composition of the local planning team on any given day, the extreme case being one day at Riverside when no teachers and 15 students greeted the agent's arrival. At Urban, teachers were available only during a 40-minute period. Late arrivals and early departures reduced effective meeting time even further. The upshot of these constraints on teachers' time was an adjustment in the planning process, either delaying some activities, rearranging others, or meeting teachers in shifts.

More typically, though, administrators posed the major time problem for field agents. In six of the schools, the principals continually bounced in and out of meetings. Because they were, at least formally, the project leaders in these schools, their absences created an acute problem for field agents: Should activities go on in the principal's absence? An affirmative answer would keep the project from sitting dead in the water, but it would also increase the field agent's leadership role. For example, the Green Hills field agent arrived one day expecting the principal to conduct the scheduled meeting, especially since several decisions that could be made only by the principal, or at least with the principal's consent, were likely to arise. The principal opened the meeting and the agent settled back to listen. After greeting everyone, the principal turned to face the agent, rose from the chair, and said while leaving the room, "why don't I leave it with you." The agent recovered from this abrupt passing of the mantle of leadership to direct the activities, especially after it became obvious that teachers would have strongly resented being called to a meeting only to have it cancelled.

In five other schools, the principal's participation was also spotty at best. However, in these cases, there was either an assistant principal, an intermediate service agency representative, or another administrator who could assume the leadership role. Only in three schools were the principals able to maintain a record of high attendance at meetings.

Time presented yet another kind of problem for the field agents. Most of the projects did not get started until the middle of the school year. By the time orientations were out of the way, only three or four months were left. Of course, it is well recognized that schools have seasons of alternately calm and frenetic activity and that one of the most frenetic is the end of the year. Unfortunately for the field agents, most of the time-consuming data collection activities necessary to select project goals occurred at the end of the year. To avoid compounding staff anxiety about closing out the school year, project activities were reshuffled, delayed, or largely taken over by RBS.

Expertise.   Expertise interacted with time to create numerous problems for field agents. At Bigtown, Oldtown, Farmcenter, Middletown, and Middleburg, at least one staff member was either familiar with project activities and content or had the time to become familiar with them. At the other schools, such expertise did not exist and time was scarce enough that no one was free to both be trained and lead the meetings. For example, the principal at Southend received training but frequently missed meetings, whereas the Neighbortown principal attended meetings but had little prior knowledge of project activities. In both cases, the field agent had to lead the group through planning sessions.

Clerical Support.   Compensating for the lack of staff time and expertise was an unwelcome but obvious responsibility that someone had to assume. Not so obviously important was the performance of seemingly simple clerical tasks. Nevertheless, providing clerical services became an integral constituent of field agents' activities in sites where such services were not readily at hand. Field agents hardly considered locating equipment, arranging for coffee, obtaining copies of documents, and providing typing to be at the heart of facilitating school change. Yet before school staff could use information to make decisions, they had to have access to it; before they could practice observing classrooms on videotapes, they had to have television monitors; and as teachers switched gears from a classroom's frantic atmosphere to the more sedate climate of a meeting, they welcomed a period of refreshments to pave the transition. In five sites (listed in Table 2), performing one or more of these clerical tasks was essential to smoothing the potentially rocky path to successful school change.

Staff Tension

Staff tensions became a second local condition that field agents had to face (second column of Table 2). The staffs in the 14 schools, as in most organizations, were not wholly united in the trouble-free pursuit of a common goal. Instead, they were divided into factions that, in varying degrees, were at odds with one another. When overt tension between factions seeped into project activities, field agents altered certain aspects of planning to reduce its effects.

At six sites, tension between teachers and administrators occasionally impinged upon the projects. When this happened, field agents intervened to keep the projects from grinding to a halt. Intervention generally consisted of mediating the conflict or, at a minimum, reducing its effects on planning. At Patriot and Suburban the agents had to go so far as to reshape the process in order to avoid tension-producing situations. Additionally at Patriot, the agent had to take over responsibilities earmarked for the principal.

Typically, tension-causing incidents surfaced outside project meetings and then threatened or directly constrained participation. For example, a Neighbortown teacher one day delivered a description of a classroom activity to the school office to be mimeographed. The principal saw the description, failed to see how it fit in with the class in which it was to be used, and subsequently questioned the teacher. The teacher responded angrily and complained to the field agent about the value of participating in the project if the principal was going to interfere with teachers' classroom decisions.

At Patriot, the principal and a planning team teacher had a dispute about the depth of detail necessary to include in instructions for substitutes. The problem had been brewing for some time and came to a head just before a planning team meeting. The teacher was upset and visibly cried throughout the meeting. Other teachers on the team knew about the incident, and they all were extremely reticent to participate, particularly when the principal was present.

In both cases, the field agent had to soften the impact of the incident so that staff would continue to participate. At

Neighbortown, the field agent knew the principal had been dealing with serious community relations that morning and explained to the teacher that because the activity in question involved a controversial issue, the principal may have thought that it was more threatening than it actually was. This interpretation of the principal's action mollified the teacher somewhat. In the Patriot case, at a break in the meeting, teachers complained to the agent that obtaining and orienting substitutes were chronic problems. They asked the agent to discuss this with the principal. The agent did so, and subsequently some adjustments were made to circumvent further conflict. Incidents like this at Patriot were frequent. Even when events ran smoothly, tensions bubbled under the surface often enough that the agent restructured some parts of the process to reduce the risk of conflict between the principal and the teachers. These changes diminished the school's overall responsibility for the project but, also, kept the teachers from withdrawing.

Staff Turnover and Disruptions to the Routine

Column 3 in Table 2 lists the schools in which field agents had to combat staff turnover and periodic disruptions. The school year, indeed the school day, in many schools is laced with regularly occurring but unplanned incidents that significantly affect school operations. In working with schools, one learns to expect the unexpected. The exact nature of an event may not be predictable, but that something will happen to change anticipated circumstances is.

In five schools, disruptive events occurred frequently enough so as to dramatically alter the configuration of field agent activities. These incidents reshaped the cast of participants and key administrators with which field agents worked. At Patriot, Urban, and Riverside, field agents were never sure of the planning team's composition from one meeting to the next. To compensate for absences of key staff, agents often had to expand their process-helping activities. The agents at Patriot, Green Hills, and Middleburg had to respond to the turnover of staff in crucial administrative positions. Consequently, they found themselves repeatedly seeking endorsements for the projects to ensure a stable flow of resources.

Incidents at Urban and Riverside illustrate how quickly unexpected occurrences could shift project leadership responsibilities in a school. On one particular day at Urban, the field agent arrived for a planning meeting only to find that the teachers' union had hastily arranged its own meeting at the same time. With only a few participants in attendance, the prospects for sparking widespread discussion were dim. As a result, the agent had to dominate the discussion much more so than was intended.

Similarly, at various times, the agent at Riverside would find the project's local coordinator and/or regular classroom teachers absent. Low teacher attendance at meetings was largely the result of chronic staff absenteeism and a shortage of substitutes. In fact, on one occasion, a planning team member missed a meeting in order to fill in for the school secretary. The field agent, of course, knew to be prepared for any contingency and, typically, wound up directing planning meetings.

Field agents at Patriot, Green Hills, and Middleburg discovered that the need to obtain administrative endorsements for the RBS projects went far beyond the period of initial entry. Administrative turnover in Patriot's district was particularly high. In the project's first two years, the district had three superintendents. The second was installed after the project had been in place for more than six months. Initially hesitant to continue it, the superintendent finally gave approval after several meetings with the field agent. However, this administration was a rocky one, and at the end of the school year, the superintendent resigned. Subsequently, the field agent embarked on a new round of obtaining endorsements.

Renegotiating endorsements was less successful for field agents at Green Hills and Middleburg, primarily because the administrators who left were the projects' key advocates. At Green Hills, the principal's replacement agreed to continue project-related activities but excused RBS from further participation. At Middleburg, the resignation of the district's curriculum coordinator weakened the principal's commitment to the project. In fact, the principal went so far as to initiate a competing school improvement effort and then explained to the field agent that the school could not afford to engage in two projects at the same time. Thus, the RBS project was dropped.

Expectations Derived from Previous Projects

The folklore surrounding in-service activities contains a myriad of stories about the faults and follies of experts—anyone "fifty miles from home." Whether based on myth or reality, staff attitudes place notable constraints on field agent activities. Such was the case in three urban schools; in the remaining schools, expectations did little to confine agents' initial behavior but played a powerful part in reinforcing the continuation of certain behaviors once exhibited.

For example, early in the Southend project, the principal took charge of at least two entire meetings. However, the principal's partial absences from subsequent meetings thrust leadership on the field agent. As time went on, the principal came to expect the agent to lead most of the sessions. At Green Hills, the principal did not call on the agent to obtain typing services until after the agent had already performed this service as (the field agent thought) a one-time means of avoiding a planning delay. Thus, agents responded to contextual conditions, and then site staff began to expect that response to be retained as part of the agents' repertoire.

At three of the urban schools, expectations loomed significant from the outset. The district regularly consulted department chairpersons at Bigtown before any kind of new program was established that affected their content area. This led the principal to include them on the planning team. However, their interest was not in actually developing the program. What they expected was that others, especially the local project coordinator and the field agent, would develop proposals for their consideration and approval. Their insistence on participating in this limited advise-and-consent capacity obliged the field agent to organize a smaller work group to do the actual program development.

Staff at both Riverside and Urban openly resented outsiders who came in to help them. "[Outsiders] get a book out of it and give the school nothing in return," said one guidance counselor at Riverside. A teacher at Urban offered another reason for the existence of disparaging opinions of outside experts. "I don't want to give you a hard time but [our] department has had 100 years of teaching experience on its staff. . . . What can you tell us that we don't know?" the teacher asked. Consequently, field agents encountered strong objections when they encouraged staff to participate. Indeed, initial planning activities got off to a slow start and picked up only after the field agent had attended to the many questions, concerns, and complaints of the teachers.

SCHOOL REACTIONS: FLEXIBILITY AND EFFECTIVENESS

This chapter began by contending that effective field agent behavior is the result of adapting agent actions to a school's context. Because local conditions differ among schools, behavior that is effective in one site may not be in another. Subsequent sections showed how field agents adjusted their behavior to counterbalance, compensate for, or accommodate to barriers to school change. Empirically it would be desirable to examine whether school change was ultimately more successful at a school where an agent matched his or her behavior to the site than where an agent did not. Realistically, though, it must be recognized that an individual's impact on a school is muted by the attitudes, beliefs, and actions of other school members as they pursue their own purposes. Indeed, the remainder of this volume pays increasing attention to the school as the primary determinant of change project outcomes. The importance of the RBS field agents resided not in their influence on final outcomes but in their ability to keep the process moving and to create conditions that increased the probability that the process would lead to the attainment of desired objectives.

School staff attested to field agent flexibility as helping to achieve these more intermediate outcomes:

> A large amount of the success of the project had to do with the field agent's ability to manage interpersonal relationships at all levels of the district.   (From a Patriot teacher)

> The field agent got teachers with a negative attitude and helped turn that around.   (From a Riverside teacher)

The field agent understood us and did not push us.   (From the Suburban principal)

In the beginning I was concerned. I felt that we wouldn't be using the field agent's expertise . . . but it didn't take too long for the field agent to see the field agent had to be involved. When the field agent became involved, the project took off. (From a Neighbortown teacher)

The above, of course, refer to instances where field agents went beyond what they had initially intended to do at a site. In schools where local staff assumed primary responsibility for leading a project, the agent's willingness to remain in the background was also noted and appreciated:

The leadership for the project was definitely from the school. When we did come up to a brick wall, RBS helped. The assistant principal did a heck of a job and was responsible for keeping it going. . . . The field agent was a good motivator and a tremendous resource.   (From an Oldtown teacher)

If we needed help and RBS was not here, there were people here trained.   (From a Smalltown Elementary teacher)

RBS got us started; I led it.   (From the Smalltown Middle assistant principal)

Interestingly, the major concern school people had about field agents was how much direction the RBS staff provided. One might expect that the schools would have jealously guarded their sovereignty over a project and that field agents would have had to tread carefully to not appear as if they were taking too much control. In fact, the opposite seemed to be true. No one really complained about too much field agent influence, but several participants did express the desire for more direction.

The principal thinks that perhaps the field agent should attempt to be a little more directive. For one thing, the members of the planning team do not know the field agent. They need to be shown that the field agent does have a lot of background knowledge and expertise; that the field agent is a capable leader.   (From the Bigtown field notes)

We needed more structure at first. Before RBS provided direction, we floundered. Finally, RBS began sharing information. . . . They made subtle suggestions and nudges. (From a Farmcenter teacher)

Or, recalling the Southend principal's words, "One cannot run an inservice and take care of everything else. What I need is for someone else to come in and do it."

SUMMARY

Agents are effective to the extent that they mold their activities to site conditions. This means occasionally expanding their responsibilities, adjusting the process, providing clerical services, obtaining reendorsements, and mediating school tensions. Rigid adherence to preconceived notions of appropriate behavior may actually work against school change.

Several additional lessons may also be drawn from this chapter. Consider the following:

- It is likely a process-helping field agent is going to have to increase his or her responsibility for leading a project, especially if principals are the major contact people.
- The timing of project activities to fit with school seasons is important. Otherwise, the process may have to be adjusted significantly.
- The planning process may increase opportunities for already-existing tensions to surface. A field agent may have to sacrifice some planning precepts for peace.
- School life is routinely disrupted. A field agent should not count too heavily on certain conditions being present for any particular activity. A plan for all, or at least some, contingencies is necessary.
- With respect to how school expectations typically reinforce field agent activities: a field agent should not do something once, if he or she is not willing to do it again.

4

The Change Process: Sequential Planning

Goals, objectives, needs assessment, and *problem solving* are all familiar terms to field agents. Generally the terms connote efforts to increase the rationality of planning activities. That is, their purpose is to optimize reasoned attainment of some desired goal. Thus, the process of decision making typically involves some variation of carefully considering what the goals of a school should be, identifying the ones that are not being met satisfactorily, and selecting methods for addressing the most important.

Many researchers, including Lindblom and Cohen (1979) and Thompson (1967), say that organizational decisions are seldom completely rational. Decision makers are not likely to have thorough knowledge of all relevant variables, to consider all the potential decision alternatives, or to be free of influence from external factors, such as community pressures or political uncertainties.

Clark (1981) makes a similar argument in the case of schools. To be sure, developers of sequential-planning procedures acknowledge that decisions will not be totally based on rational considerations. Nevertheless, at a minimum, they believe that orderly collection of data and deliberation about what the data say should help discipline decision making, and thereby enhance the quality of plans. That this belief is widely held in education is reflected in the numerous school improvement efforts that rely on variants of sequential planning (e.g., school improvement programs in California, Pennsylvania, and Virginia).

This chapter is about the use of sequential planning in the RBS projects. The extent to which groups went through the process and made decisions on the basis of prescribed information varied from school to school. Often this depended upon local conditions, particularly the availability of resources, customary decision-making practices, compatibility between school and project priorities, and school factions. First, the chapter briefly discusses the pervasiveness of sequential-planning models, the reasons why people support such models, and the way in which the RBS projects used sequential-planning procedures. Then, it traces how school contextual conditions interacted with the planning process. The chapter concludes by suggesting tactics to help field agents reconcile the inherent tug-of-war between sequential planning and local conditions.

THE PERVASIVENESS OF SEQUENTIAL PLANNING

Sequential-planning procedures are built into many models or approaches described in the literature on educational innovation and curriculum development. For example, the problem-solving (Paul, 1977) and linkage (Havelock, 1973) approaches to school change both include identification of problems or needs, selection of solutions from various alternatives, and implementation of the solutions. Systematically collected data help identify needs and select alternatives most likely to be effective. The authors of classic works on curriculum development (e.g., Smith, Stanley, and Shores, 1957; Taba, 1962; and Tyler, 1949) view sequential planning as a process that includes considering the goals or directions of education, assessing their attainment, and judging how they can be met most effectively.

Researchers have duly noted that planning is seldom as rational as it is intended to be (Allison, 1971; Berman, 1981; March and Simon, 1958; Paul, 1977). For example, a decision to adopt an innovation is sometimes more an opportunistic grasp for extra funds than it is a carefully thought-out response to an identified need (Greenwood, Mann, and McLaughlin,

1975). At other times, curriculum decisions may be made informally and piecemeal without careful consideration of alternatives and consequences (Kirst and Walker, 1971). If, and how, a sequential planning process is used may be influenced by the availability of release time for teachers (Rosenblum and Louis, 1981), the ambiguity of educational goals and the difficulty of assessing their attainment (Miles, 1981), the existence of relatively autonomous subunits with competing needs and interests (Rosenblum and Louis, 1981), and community controversy or antagonism (Paul, 1977). In general, there is growing recognition that the assumptions underlying most approaches to sequential planning do not adequately reflect the reality of educational organizations (Clark, 1981).

PERCEIVED ADVANTAGES OF SEQUENTIAL PLANNING

Supporters of sequential-planning strategies point out several advantages. First, sequential planning leads to the selection of changes that are appropriate and feasible for a particular setting because decisions will have been made on the basis of perceived local needs and knowledge of resource constraints. People who are familiar with a setting will have considered several alternatives before selecting the topics they consider best to address. Second, the rational planning process helps to develop support for and commitment to the changes selected. During a group's decision-making process, a consensus will have likely been built. This reassures members about the soundness of their decision and commits them to carrying out the innovation (March and Simon, 1958; Paul, 1977). Third, participants are less likely to discontinue using the innovation after initial incentives are withdrawn (Zaltman, Florio, and Sikorski, 1977). The reason they implemented a change in the first place was that they believed it would improve instruction, not because someone else offered a temporary incentive. Fourth, the process of comparing desired goals with current conditions helps overcome a natural resistance to change by convincing participants that their present situation is unsatisfactory (March and Simon, 1958; Zaltman et al., 1977).

SEQUENTIAL PLANNING IN THE RBS PROJECTS

This section describes how the sequential-planning process was applied to basic skills, career education, and citizen education. The basic skills approach involved training participants to collect data on classroom practices; comparing classroom data to research-based data and setting improvement goals; selecting strategies to address those goals; planning implementation; deciding how to evaluate the changes; and implementing the strategies. Information from each phase of the process was to be used in the next phase.

The career education approach included identifying program goals; conducting needs assessment surveys of faculty members, community members, and students; identifying resources available in the school and community; identifying priority goals to be implemented; designing a program; implementing it; and evaluating it.

The citizenship education approach was similar. It had three phases. The first phase consisted of nine "tasks": organizing a school improvement team, orienting it, establishing goals for citizen education, identifying sources of data and instrumentation, setting performance criteria, observing citizen education behaviors, assessing observational results, refining performance criteria, and developing a formal needs statement. The second phase used information from the first phase in program development and implementation. The third phase focused on program evaluation.

The degree to which schools adhered to the sequential processes varied. Table 3 characterizes planning at each site, along with the local factors that influenced it. In column 3 the table shows whether the planning group (1) carried out all stages of the planning process and (2) allowed the process to guide their decision-making behavior. The first set of characteristics indicate whether the process was followed at least until decisions about what changes to implement had been made. Obviously a planning procedure cannot be expected to affect implementation if those using it never reach the final step of deciding what to implement. The second set of characteristics is important because a group cannot be considered to have really used a particular planning process if its decisions were not

TABLE 3. Summary of the Nature of the Sequential-Planning Process and Local Conditions

Site	Project	Nature of Sequential-Planning Process	Factors That Facilitated Planning	Factors That Interfered with Planning
Middleburg	Basic skills	Process discontinued before commitment to specific changes Suggested changes vetoed by administrator	Resources available to hire substitutes Project and school goals compatible	Initial incentives for participation ended School adopted new program viewed as incompatible with project
Middletown	Basic skills	Process enacted except for wrap-up meetings Some changes implemented prematurely	Resources available to hire substitutes Project goals of high priority to school	Time demands considered too high Ordinary knowledge used to make project-related decisions
Patriot	Basic skills	Process enacted Data collection procedures altered Some changes made without being identified as important by data	Resources available to hire substitutes Project and school goals highly compatible	Time demands considered too high Substitute teachers perceived as incompetent Factions existed between staff and administrators Teachers used ordinary knowledge to identify problems rather than the planning process; also, some major problems beyond scope of innovation

Smalltown Elementary	Basic skills	Entire process enacted	Project and school goals compatible Teacher evaluation system used to provide incentives Staff time available	
Smalltown Middle	Basic skills	Entire process enacted	Project and school goals compatible Teacher evaluation system used to provide incentives Staff time available	
Southend	Basic skills	Entire process enacted	Project and school goals compatible Teacher evaluation system used to provide incentives	Time demands considered too high, especially in second year
Bigtown	Career preparation	Entire process enacted	Initial planning team members had light teaching loads Resources available to hire other teachers to write implementation plans Staff member available with time and incentives to pursue career education State mandate to implement career education	Project and school goals not highly compatible

(continued on next page)

TABLE 3 (Continued)

Site	Project	Nature of Sequential-Planning Process	Factors That Facilitated Planning	Factors That Interfered with Planning
Green Hills	Career preparation	Entire process enacted Scope of planned changes limited New principal negated process decisions	Separate resources available to support development of specific implementation plans	Proctoring arrangement aroused resistance among nonparticipants Innovation goals given low priority, threatened other goals
Neighbortown	Career preparation	Entire process enacted Scope of planned changes limited Goal priorities not used in implementation plans	Separate resources available to support development of specific implementation plans	Administrators not willing to use resources to pay teachers for after-school project work Project goals given low priority, threatened other goals
Oldtown	Career preparation	Revised planning process enacted	State grant provided resources to enact process, and obligations to do so State mandate to implement career education	Other time demands distracted key person from project initially Project goals given low priority initially
Farmcenter	Citizen education	Entire process enacted Low-intensity changes recommended	Staff time to participate available	Resources not available to support later process enactment Project and school goals not highly compatible
Riverside	Citizen education	Process discontinued before implementation plans made		Resources not available to support process enactment

			Project and school goals not highly compatible
			Factions between teachers and administrators and between teachers and students delayed progress
			RBS assistance reduced before implementation plans completed
Suburban	Citizen education	Process discontinued after needs assessment stage	Resources not available to support enactment
			Project goals of low priority in school
			Project goals threatened system goals by impinging on nonparticipants
			RBS assistance reduced before implementation planning completed
Urban	Citizen education	Process discontinued before implementation plans made	Resources not available to support enactment
			Project goals of low priority in school
			Factions delayed progress during meetings
			RBS assistance reduced before implementation planning completed

based on data or were not made at an appropriate time. The planning procedures were to give participants a framework for making their decisions. If they made decisions without paying much attention to the process, it can be said that they used the process ritualistically and were not influenced by it.

LOCAL SCHOOL CONDITIONS AND SEQUENTIAL PLANNING

Several factors explain why some schools were able to work through the sequential process and make their decisions fairly easily and some were not. First, securing necessary resources, particularly the time participants needed to meet with one another, was highly problematic in some schools. This seriously affected the relative emphasis given to different activities in the planning sequence. Second, in making decisions about what changes were needed, most participants continued to use the ordinary, or common-sense, knowledge that steered their everyday practice rather than using knowledge from the planning process. Teachers, especially, seemed to view more scientifically based knowledge in the same way Waller (1967) regarded sociological thought in his day, "A sociological writer cannot, in the present state of our science, hope to get very far ahead of common sense, and he is usually fortunate if he does not fall behind it" (p. 3). Third, the compatibility between school and project priorities varied considerably. When they were incompatible, people were less willing to devote resources to planning or consider changes as extensive as those suggested by the process. Fourth, factions within some schools made it difficult for groups to conduct reasoned discussions or to cooperate in planning efforts. RBS' involvement in the projects was still another factor that influenced planning. When its assistance was withdrawn before participants reached the point of deciding what changes to implement, they were unlikely to continue the process themselves.

The following discussions of school-context factors that affected planning are necessarily brief. Each of the five sections could easily be given a chapter's space. At times, this brevity may provide a somewhat choppy view of the planning process. The reader may want to return to Appendix A from time to time to get a more complete sense of events at each school.

School Resources

The sequential-planning process made huge time demands on school staff. Each step took many hours to complete, pulling teachers and administrators away from their regular duties. Indeed, the time that teachers normally set aside for classroom clerical chores was used to (1) discuss and agree on definitions and goals, (2) develop, administer, and analyze needs-assessment results, (3) establish goal priorities, (4) learn to conduct classroom observations, (5) observe instructional lessons, (6) complete forms specifying the contents of curricula and achievement tests, and (7) interpret data.

More time to plan was available in some sites than others. In most schools where the majority of participants had regular classroom teaching assignments, time for project activities was particularly limited. School personnel without teaching assignments or with lighter work loads were able to adjust their schedules more readily than teachers and could attend meetings free of the need for substitutes. Some could even absorb process tasks into their regular duties, as was the case of a district administrator in charge of Bigtown's own career education program. At least one participant in every school was an administrator, a guidance counselor, or a specialist. Because of their more flexible schedules, these people sometimes assumed key roles in the project by making logistical arrangements for meetings and other activities.

Monetary resources were important to helping schools cope with time requirements. For the most part, funds made it possible to hire substitute teachers. As in the case of time, the availability of this resource varied among schools. Only two schools, Patriot and Middletown, were able to hire substitutes to release teachers for all project meetings. The Patriot funds were supplied by the school district; the funds used in Middletown were secured by an intermediate service agency from the state department. Limited monetary resources were available

in eight other sites (all except Farmcenter, Suburban, Riverside, and Urban) to occasionally hire substitute teachers or pay
participants for project activities.

When monetary resources were not sufficient to hire substitutes, other arrangements were made to release teachers from
regular responsibilities. One type of arrangement involved
asking nonparticipants in the school to proctor participants'
classes. This occurred at both Green Hills and Neighbortown.
A second type of arrangement was to either schedule project
meetings during periods when several participants had no
teaching assignments or, conversely, select participants according to who had free periods when project meetings were
scheduled. A third type of arrangement was to hold meetings
after school. Occasionally some combination of the above was
used.

Meeting the resource requirements of the sequential-planning process had several side effects on how a planning group
went through the sequence of activities. One of these was that
available money and time would sometimes be consumed before participants had a chance to discuss or implement new
practices. When this happened, field agents would have to
compress the latter stages. Participants viewed this as unfortu-
nate because, to them, these stages were the most useful portions of the process, especially given the limited time teachers
normally have to share ideas with one another. At Middletown,
for example, approximately five meetings were devoted to
procedures for conducting observations and analyzing data;
only two were spent in discussing implementation strategies
and deciding which new practices to implement. This happened because by the time the group had reached the point of
considering new practices, the field agents had become aware
that resources would be depleted soon and, so, accelerated the
process.

Current Decision-Making Practices

Using a sequential-planning strategy to decide what changes to
implement required participants to depart considerably from
their usual modes of behavior. Although participants were
familiar with the process of identifying a problem, considering

alternatives, and selecting the most effective or feasible for implementation, in practice such decisions were apt to be made informally and privately. Furthermore, people were more likely to turn to common-sense knowledge rather than to systematically collected information to make classroom decisions. Their decisions and behavior, consequently, were often influenced more by familiar patterns of behavior than by planning activities. Some participants also implemented changes individually before the group as a whole had reached the stage of deciding what changes to make.

The distinction between the common-sense knowledge that participants customarily used and the more systematically collected information obtained during the planning process is similar to the distinction between *ordinary* and *scientific* knowledge (Campbell, 1974; Schuetz, 1953). People accept ordinary or common-sense knowledge as true without evidence that it has been systematically generated or validated. Such knowledge is gradually assimilated through experience or prescriptions for effective professional practice (for example, "tell students immediately what you expect of them" and "don't smile until December"). Scientific knowledge has also been labeled "professional social inquiry" (Lindblom and Cohen, 1979) and "research-based knowledge" (Louis, 1981). It refers in this section to knowledge generated through or gathered for use in the planning procedures—for example, data from the career education and citizenship education needs assessments, the basic skills research base, or time-on-task observations. The terms *procedural* and *process* are used here as synonyms for that type of knowledge.

Ordinary knowledge, of course, will be used to some extent at virtually all stages of any planning process. It will play a role in establishing objectives, designing needs assessments, and developing implementation plans. Ordinary knowledge that is of particular interest here is that which modified or replaced procedural knowledge, either during the designated stage of the process or before it. (The reader should keep in mind that the authors do not intentionally attach negative connotations to participants' use of ordinary knowledge in favor of more systematically derived information.)

When teachers at Patriot selected strategies for increasing

time-on-task, they used their ordinary knowledge to adjust the observation data. The observations showed that most student off-task behavior was in the management/transition category. However, the teachers had long believed that lack of discipline was the most serious problem in the school. They decided that improving discipline (which the data indicated was a lesser problem), therefore, would increase time-on-task more than reducing management/transition time.

Participants also used ordinary knowledge to decide whether to use research knowledge presented by field agents. Basic skills field agents, for example, distributed research summaries to help participants select strategies to increase time-on-task. One of these findings that field agents and participants brought up repeatedly in meetings was that time-on-task was higher during large-group instruction than during small-group or individualized instruction. Some teachers changed their grouping patterns accordingly; many others did not. The latter teachers continued to believe that individualized and small-group instruction was better.

Sequential planning specified that participants were to decide what classroom changes to implement either after doing observations and analyzing the data or after assessing needs and assigning priorities to goals. However, teachers sometimes implemented changes before either of the activities had taken place. Participants in the basic skills projects identified changes that would increase time-on-task throughout the process, even during the earliest stages. One Middletown teacher said that while looking at videotapes used for observation training, the realization struck that a lot of learning time was wasted when students waited in line to see the teacher, receive or hand in assignments, or be dismissed. Other teachers commented that they became aware of strategies for reducing transition time when they informally exchanged ideas during training, saw strategies used by other teachers, and listened to the comments and suggestions of people who observed their classrooms. The teachers saw little reason to wait weeks until reaching the designated stage of the process to implement changes when they had already discovered an idea that could increase time-on-task and improve classroom atmosphere.

The above examples are all drawn from basic skills sites; in the career education projects, participants rarely did anything independently of the process. They made few classroom changes before the group had reached the designated stage, and they made greater use of procedural knowledge to make decisions. A similar phenomenon appeared to take place in the citizen education sites. However, the short time span of these projects made such comparisons more difficult to establish.

These differences in RBS' basic skills and career education projects appeared to be primarily due to several factors. First, basic skills participants were experienced at making decisions about instruction in math and reading. Many career education participants were unfamiliar with the concept of career education; their ordinary knowledge was not adequate to make decisions or stimulate implementation. While the early process stages gave teachers some ideas about implementation, these notions were not well formed.

Second, incentives for implementation were high for teachers in the basic skills projects (in the form of relatively immediate effects on student performance) but low for teachers in the career education projects. The career education participants perceived few rewards aside from the motivational value of doing something different. They also faced a few disincentives in the form of nonparticipating colleagues who might disapprove if participants spent class time on career education at the expense of regular subject matter content.

Third, career education implementation required considerable effort. Teachers had to locate or write career-related activities and then prepare them for presentation to students. Implementation of the basic skills changes required relatively little preparation; they easily meshed with already ongoing practices. Moreover, most of the career education activities would be used only once with a particular class; the basic skills strategies improved classroom conditions over a long period of time.

School and Project Priorities

Sequential planning was sometimes constrained by competition between project objectives and other school priorities, like adhering to curricula and maintaining harmonious relationships with the community and among staff members. Such priorities interfered with the process more in the career education and citizenship education projects than in basic skills where there was generally high consensus about the importance of the project goals.

Sometimes conflict between project and school priorities limited the scope of changes decided upon, even when data suggested more ambitious changes were needed to meet project objectives. For example, participants in Neighbortown and Green Hills avoided changes that might jeopardize coverage of content area topics. Participants decided to "infuse" career education into regular subjects rather than replace content-area curricula with career education materials. Other methods of addressing project goals included adding courses and sponsoring special activities such as resource centers, which also did not interfere with regular content coverage.

Priorities regarding relationships between school and community interfered with change decisions at these same two sites. Participants in Green Hills and Neighbortown wanted to plan career education activities that would involve the community—by arranging out-of-school experiences for students and bringing community members into the schools. Administrators reported they were afraid that these activities could arouse community resistance to the project and injure community-school relationships, especially if students misbehaved. As a result, they vetoed the ideas.

In two cases, project planning was affected by administrators trying to maintain harmony among staff members. The principal at Suburban sometimes truncated project activities to reduce resistance from nonparticipants. They had been asked to donate planning time to help construct the needs assessment. Several resented that and reported it to the local teachers' association. When substitutes were not available at Patriot, the principal reduced project meeting time rather than ask other teachers to cover for participants.

At Green Hills, all stages of the sequential-planning process were carried out, but final change decisions were rescinded by a new principal who wanted to address other priorities. Furthermore, the project had aroused resistance among nonparticipants, partly because of the attention it was given. The principal wanted to defuse that resistance in order to establish a good relationship with the faculty. Career education could not be totally discontinued, however, because the central office said that a program should be developed. The principal decided to meet that mandate expediently so that time could then be devoted to other goals. This was done by discontinuing the ongoing effort (including the sequential-planning process, RBS' involvement, and the planning team), which the principal perceived was delaying progress, and by assigning the task of writing career education curriculum materials to members of a faculty council.

Of course, other school priorities were not always at odds with those of the RBS projects. For example, one school had an employee whom district administrators expected to develop a career education curriculum. The project goals were, of course, quite compatible with the employee's. The person not only needed to develop a curriculum, but also sought the kinds of assistance RBS offered. As a result, the person was willing to devote a great deal of time to sequential planning. That district and another were located in a state where, during the course of the project, the state education agency mandated career education. This heightened the importance of career education goals. The mandate, then, facilitated the process by boosting the priority of career education as a system goal.

Factions

Factions within school faculties and between teachers and administrators can have many effects on the planning process. Competition for resources or recognition, for example, can easily thwart cooperative efforts. Some of the effects of within-school tensions on the RBS project have already have been described. Tensions between participants and nonparticipants sometimes made the former hesitant to devote time to the process or to attempt changing regular content-area curricula. Fear of provoking tensions sometimes led administrators to limit project efforts. By and large, though, these tensions were minor and were created by the projects; this section is primarily concerned with school factions that existed before a project was introduced.

In Riverside and Urban, both urban secondary schools, factions developed and gained strength as the schools underwent strikes. Moreover, teachers found ways to circumvent the wishes of administrators they viewed as weak. It became a struggle in both schools to enlist participants willing to exert the effort required to carry out the process. Also, discussions of program philosophy and goals were frequently reduced to opportunities for people to vent ongoing frustrations with the schools in general. These led to heated arguments far removed from reasoned discussions about the specific school improvement project at hand.

Factions between teachers and administrators (both at the school and in the central office) at Patriot diluted the emphasis given to certain process activities. Administrators had originally planned to help conduct classroom observations. However, teachers would not tolerate them in that role and chose, instead, to observe one another's classrooms. With less time available for observations, fewer were conducted. Field agents reported that this may have weakened the reliability of the data used to make decisions.

A Note on Continued Assistance from RBS

The sequential-planning process was also influenced by the continuation of assistance from RBS employees. In several sites, RBS assistance was seriously curtailed or completely withdrawn because of funding cuts before the process had been put into full operation. Because field agents provided several kinds of assistance during the process (Chapter 3), some schools became highly dependent on them. When their assistance was cut short or eliminated somewhat abruptly the process was unlikely to continue.

RBS assistance was withdrawn in three citizen education sites—Urban, Riverside, and Suburban—before participants were able to decide what changes to implement. None of those sites completed the process. In each, serious impediments to planning existed. Resources to support the process were not

available in any of the sites; the project goal, citizenship education, was of relatively low priority; factions existed among
faculty members and between them and administrators; in
addition, there were few incentives for continuing the process.
Thus, without the constant urging and encouragement of field
agents, the projects fell by the wayside.

Field agents in citizen education also withdrew their assistance from their fourth site, Farmcenter, but there the process
continued. Farmcenter shared some, but not all, of the problems of the three other sites. Few resources were available to
facilitate planning, and the project's major goal was of relatively low priority. However, factions were not a serious problem in the school. More importantly, the principal had a keen
interest in the project and scheduled time for related activities.
Finally, the planning process had progressed further there at
the time that RBS had to withdraw. Planning teams had already
begun to discuss what changes to implement and, therefore,
had less to do to complete the process.

RBS assistance also ended in a fifth site, Middleburg, before
planning had been completed. However, the decision to discontinue the project at this basic skills site was made by site
participants rather than by RBS.

IMPLICATIONS

From the preceding discussion, it is clear that uninterrupted
sequential planning is more possible in some schools than
others. Factors that influence the sequencing of planning activities or the extent to which planning activities guide decisions
include the availability of resources, the current practices of
participants in making classroom decisions, the compatibility of
school and project priorities, and the existence of factions
within schools.

Although the barriers facing projects that use sequential
planning are considerable, field agents can do much to help
planning groups carry out the process successfully. If they are
alert to the potential influences of local school conditions, field
agents can construct ways to counteract them. Strategies to

reduce the influence of *resource availability* include the following:

- Obtain resources to pay substitutes or otherwise release or remunerate teachers.
- See that meetings are scheduled well in advance so that substitutes can be obtained and arrange for the same substitutes to work in the same classroom each time.
- Avoid frequent meetings when people are busy with other activities.
- Intensify the process during its early stages, allowing participants to see progress while they are still enthusiastic.
- Avoid spending too much time on particular parts of the process and making it necessary to slight other parts.
- Eliminate or drastically reduce tasks that are of marginal utility.

To reduce the influence of *current decision-making practices*, field agents can

- Give participants the opportunity to make reasoned decisions early in the process. If some people perceive a need for and want to make changes before the designated stage of the process, discuss their perceptions of conditions, needs, and changes that might be made tentatively until the data are available.
- Minimize the amount of time it takes to acquire data. Avoid lengthy preparation processes for data collection and long delays before data are available for use.
- Make sure that people are comfortable with the information on which they are to base decisions: Do they understand it thoroughly? Is it credible to them—accurate, representative, a valid indicator of an important construct?
- Legitimize the use of other information in decisions. After the data are available, discuss whether or not people think they are worthy of use in decision making and what other factors need to be considered.

The following are suggested to reduce the influence of *competing school priorities:*

- Establish school and project goal compatibility at the beginning of a project and select innovations and schools partially on the basis of goal compatibility. If project goals are of low priority in comparison to other school goals, make sure that administrators are firmly committed to the project and that other staff are aware of that commitment.
- Identify individuals for whom project goals are most important and recruit them as early supporters.
- Monitor effects of the planning process on the school and adjust the process when it impinges on the operation of the remainder of the school.
- Look for ways in which the process can address important school goals—for example, help meet a new state mandate or community concern—and bring that to people's attention.

Developing a similar list of recommendations to minimize the influence of *factions* is difficult. Field agents can use group process techniques and, to the extent they consider wise, follow some of the suggestions listed below. However, openly discussing conflicts and grievances can have negative as well as positive effects. Field agents must judge which effects are likely to result.

- Structure discussions that involve issues likely to aggravate group frictions so that concerns can be aired but will not altogether block further planning.
- Avoid overrepresentation of a single faction so that others will not identify the project solely with them.
- Work behind the scenes to obtain information on what causes tension in a school and take this into account when planning meeting activities.
- Meet privately with faction leaders to address questions they have about the project and how the project may help *professional* concerns they have.

5 | The Change Process: Local Participation

It has become customary to involve teachers who will implement an innovation in its early planning stages. Such involvement was stimulated by applied research conducted in the 1930s and 1940s (Coch and French, 1948). Since then, it has become pretty much the rule, boosted by a Rand Corporation report (Berman and McLaughlin, 1977), that teacher participation is a critical factor in the successful implementation and continuation of changes. According to the Rand study, teacher involvement enhances local commitment and motivation as well as builds capacity to use an innovation. It can also ensure that any changes will be appropriate for the local setting.

Despite the apparent benefits of local participation, there are still some situations where its costs may hamper success. Participation diverts staff time and energy from regular duties. If demands are high and either the payoff is not easily visible or regular responsibilities suffer, then local commitment, capacity, and adaptation may never occur. Thus, field agents must constantly balance the costs of participation with the benefits.

In fact, teacher participation may not be a realistic expectation in all schools, or at least not in the same form. The extent to which people are willing and able to become actively involved in educational innovation is influenced by several local school conditions: the availability of resources, incentives and disincentives perceived by participants, and school tensions.

Resources, such as staff time to plan or money for hiring substitutes, constrain the number of people who can be involved and for what length of time; incentives and disincentives affect people's willingness to shift their energy to a project; and tensions can create a meeting atmosphere that is counterproductive to planning, thereby discouraging some staff from becoming involved.

This chapter explores the factors that influenced teacher participation in the RBS planning groups. It also looks at how well such participation met its objective of building local commitment to change. First, though, there is a brief review of the literature on the rationale for participation and its nature in the projects. Then, after tracing the influences of local conditions on participation, the chapter discusses process adjustments that reduced the influence of the factors. Finally, there is an examination of the influence of those adjustments on the effects of participation.

WHY ENCOURAGE PARTICIPATION?

The term *participation* refers to formal opportunities for teachers to be present during the process of making decisions about school improvement (Firestone, 1977). The extent to which participants actually influence decisions can vary substantially. People may (1) simply provide information that others will use to make decisions, (2) voice opinions and make recommendations—which may or may not be taken into consideration, (3) vote upon or veto decisions suggested by administrators, or (4) make decisions with no distinction between themselves and administrators (Dachler and Wilpert, 1978; Devlin, 1981; Giacquinta, 1973). The scope of these decisions can vary from minor changes in a teacher's classroom to major school-wide policy changes.

The literature contains three major underlying reasons for involving local participants in planning. First, participation increases people's commitment (or at least willingness) to spend the time and effort required to implement new practices and to continue them after initial incentives are withdrawn (Berman and McLaughlin, 1977; Firestone and Corbett, 1979). Those who help plan an innovation are likely to develop psychological ownership of it and to persevere rather than waste the resources already invested in it (Bartunek and Keys, 1979; Mann, 1978). The group setting of participation can reduce resistance and generate a sense of public commitment to an innovation (Havelock, 1973; Katz and Kahn, 1966).

Second, participation helps develop local capacity for implementation; that is, people will acquire the knowledge and skills needed to change their behavior (Gross, Giacquinta, and Bernstein, 1971; McLaughlin and Marsh, 1978). They are more likely to thoroughly understand a program when they are exposed to its developmental process and know the reasons that led to certain decisions. Furthermore, they may have an opportunity to receive technical assistance from external experts and to have blocks of time specifically allocated to knowledge and skill acquisition.

Third, local participation in project planning heightens the possibility that changes will be appropriate in a particular setting (Bartunek and Keys, 1979; Berman and McLaughlin, 1977). Teachers tend to know more about a setting, its needs, and the kinds of improvements that are feasible than external experts. Even if an innovation has been partially developed in advance, teachers can provide feedback and suggest corrections or modifications (Berman and McLaughlin, 1977).

Research on participation has been less clear about its effects. Some reviewers of the literature say that participation indeed helps create commitment and ownership (Havelock, 1973; Paul, 1977). Others, however, claim that research findings are generally inconclusive (Fullan and Pomfret, 1977; Giacquinta, 1973). Suggested explanations for the different findings are that (1) the studies used varied or unclear definitions of participation and different methodologies and (2) reviewers used different literature bases and examined the literature from different perspectives (Felker and Davis, 1979; Giacquinta, 1973).

One reason for the inconsistency of research findings about participation may be that its effects, as well as the extent to which it can be carried out, vary among settings. However, relatively little is known about this issue. For example, some researchers (e.g., Sieber, 1981) have noted that participation is very demanding on resources, but they have not dealt with the implications of this for schools with different amounts of resources. This chapter argues that school context has significant effects on participation and its intended benefits. More specifically, it examines (1) how the availability of resources, incentives and disincentives, and interpersonal tensions influenced the nature of participation and (2) whether participation led to the development of a strong commitment to the innovation process and the resulting changes. The other two often-stated benefits of encouraging participation, building capacity and tailoring the innovation to a site, were more difficult to assess precisely and, thus, receive only brief attention in this chapter.

PARTICIPATION IN THE RBS PROJECTS

Soon after the project was initiated in each school, administrators designated a planning team, either by appointing participants or asking for volunteers. Members of the team were to attend project meetings and conduct planning activities. Through these activities, they would develop a new program. Team members included classroom teachers, administrators, other school and district personnel (e.g., guidance counselors and curriculum specialists), and sometimes community members or students. Meetings were held during or after school and varied in length from less than one hour to an entire day. Classroom teachers were able to attend meetings held during the school day because substitutes or colleagues covered their classes or because meetings occurred during planning periods. Table 4 identifies planning team members in each school and summarizes the meeting arrangements.

The methods used to develop plans and the activities of participants varied across the three RBS content areas (Dawson, 1979). In the career education and citizen education projects, teams initially worked in groups as they went through a sequential-planning process. This process encouraged partic-

TABLE 4. Initial Planning Team Size, Composition, and Meeting Arrangements

School	Number of People on Team	Composition of Initial Planning Team	Time of Meetings	Duration of Meetings	Arrangements for Teachers to Attend In-School Meetings
Middleburg	10	7 teachers, reading specialist, principal, district-level supervisor	During or after school	70 minutes to all day	Substitutes hired—money from intermediate agency
Middletown	9	6 teachers, reading specialist, counselor, principal	During school	Half day or all day	Substitutes hired—money from intermediate agency
Patriot	5	4 teachers, principal	During school	Half day or all day	Substitutes hired—money from district; when substitutes unavailable, others covered classes or meetings shortened
Smalltown Elementary	7	4 teachers, specialist, assistant principal, principal	During or after school	1 hour to all day	Substitutes hired—money from other special projects
Smalltown Middle	6	4 teachers, assistant principal, principal	During or after school	1 hour to all day	Substitutes hired—money from other special projects
Southend	4	3 teachers, principal	During or after school	1 hour to all day	Substitutes hired—money from other special projects

Bigtown	13	1 teacher, 4 department chairpersons, counselor, career education coordinator, principal, assistant superintendent, 2 students, teacher from a feeder school, community members	During school	1–2 hours	Most were chairpersons with released time
Green Hills	13	4 teachers, counselor, principal, assistant superintendent, community members	During school	1–3 hours	Nonparticipant proctors
Neighbortown	8	2 teachers, counselor, principal, assistant superintendent, student, community members	During school	2 hours	Nonparticipant proctors; some substitutes used
Oldtown	9	3 teachers, counselor, vice-principal, principal, 2 district-level employees, community member	During school	All day	Substitutes

(continued on next page)

TABLE 4 (Continued)

School	Number of People on Team	Composition of Initial Planning Team	Time of Meetings	Duration of Meetings	Arrangements for Teachers to Attend In-School Meetings
Farmcenter	At least 12	At least 4 teachers, 3 students, guidance counselor, assistant principal, principal, 2 or 3 parents. Also, several representatives of community agencies attended meetings; team status unknown.	During or after school	80 minutes–2½ hours	Unknown for in-school meetings
Riverside	More than 10 at each meeting	"Team" not specifically identified; meetings attended by 2–4 teachers, 0–3 grade-level chairpersons, 0–22 students, 1–6 community members	During school	65–90 minutes	Few teachers attended; chairpersons had lighter loads
Suburban	At least 10	3 teachers, department chairperson, principal, at least 3 community members, 2–3 students	During school	65 minutes–4 hours	Nonparticipant proctors
Urban	At least 10	At least 5 teachers, department chairperson, intern, coach, assistant principal, principal	During school	40 minutes	Planning periods

ipants to identify goals and objectives, conduct needs assessment surveys, use the survey results to prioritize goals, and develop school-level plans. Field agents suggested alternatives and offered advice. Participants generally made most of the decisions, although administrators sometimes indicated that options being considered were unacceptable to them, school board members, or the local community. Teachers developed classroom-level plans individually or in small groups.

In the basic skills projects, participants received training in data collection and analysis procedures, carried them out, and then decided what changes to make. A few of those decisions extended beyond individual classrooms (e.g., to revise schedules), but most did not. During the entire process, team members tended to work independently more than as a group. They went through the same procedures at the same time and talked to one another, but individually completed practice exercises, collected and analyzed data, and selected classroom-level changes. Planning teams seldom made group decisions or collectively developed program plans.

THE INFLUENCE OF LOCAL SCHOOL CONDITIONS ON PARTICIPATION

As anyone who has worked in a school well knows, participation in extra projects does not come cheaply. Trade-offs between being involved and performing regular duties must continually be made. How heavy those demands were, and the effects they had, varied among the 14 schools. The major local school contextual conditions that affected participation were the availability of resources, incentives and disincentives for participation, and the existence of tensions within schools. Table 5 summarizes the important factors in each site.

The Availability of Resources

Developing program plans was a lengthy process, and time was scarce in all schools, although more so in some than others. The lack of time was particularly a problem in the elementary

TABLE 5. Local School Conditions That Influenced Participation

School	Resources	Incentives	Disincentives	Tensions
Middletown	Elementary school; teachers had full schedules Key participant was specialist with ambition, flexible time Assistant principal responsible for many routine administrative matters Money from regional service agency to pay substitutes Field agent from regional service agency willing to assume many leadership responsibilities	Achievement test scores low Contact with other teachers, professionals	Project required considerable time; substitutes not always satisfactory Previous innovations dropped prematurely	Some tensions between teachers, specialist, and administrators
Patriot	Elementary school; teachers had full schedules District money to pay substitutes, but they were not always available	Achievement test scores low; school given provisional status by state	Project required considerable time; substitutes sometimes not available or considered incompetent, parents complained	High tensions between teachers and administrators
Riverside			Participants skeptical that their input would be used, that changes would occur Suspicion of "hidden agenda" from RBS; fearful of federal intervention	Tensions in school and district over contracts and layoffs; High rate of teacher absenteeism
Urban			Participants skeptical that RBS could assist inner-city school	Tensions among faculty, with community and students, racial overtones

School				
Farmcenter	Planning team included principal, assistant principal, and counselor, all with flexible schedules. Principal willing to assume project leadership	Incentives unknown, but evidence suggests that principal was looked upon as innovator	New projects begun that reduced enthusiasm for RBS	Appeared to be low
Oldtown	Planning team included a counselor and 4 administrators, all with flexible schedules. Vice principal willing to assume project leadership. Grant from state	State graduation requirement plans could be fulfilled through project. Activity-writing team paid. Grant money had to be used for project	Coordinator very busy; other responsibilities often had priority	Light tension
Smalltown Elementary	Elementary school; teachers had full schedules	Innovation procedures incorporated into teacher evaluation. In-service credit	Project required considerable time	Appeared to be low
Smalltown Middle	No evidence that time was a serious problem	Innovation procedures incorporated into teacher evaluation. In-service credit		
Southend	Elementary school; teachers had full schedules. Some money from other special projects to pay substitutes. School involved in several special projects at the same time	Achievement test scores lowest in district. Innovation procedures incorporated into teacher evaluation. Superintendent strong supporter of project. In-service credit	Project required considerable time	Appeared to be low

(continued on next page)

TABLE 5 (Continued)

School	Resources	Incentives	Disincentives	Tensions
Green Hills	Grant from state Teacher time limited but flexible	Students scored low on career education section of state achievement test Several participants had prior involvement with career education Teachers expected to participate in at least one special project	Fear of not meeting other responsibilities Resentment from non-participants who were repeatedly asked to proctor	Tensions between administrator's group (some on planning team) and others
Middleburg	Elementary school; teachers had full schedules 2 team members were administrators, one a specialist Money from regional service agency to pay substitutes	Few incentives for teachers Initial incentives for administrators (career possibilities for one, friendship obligations for the other) ceased after one year	Participants' suggestion of changes to make were rejected by principal	Tensions between teachers, specialist, and administrators
Neighbortown	Planning team included a counselor and 2 administrators, with flexible schedules Grant from state	Administrator interested in career education; also saw project as opportunity to get money for school; teachers flattered by being picked		Light tension

Suburban		Principal wanted to develop leadership skills Some participants concerned about lack of citizenship (e.g., failure to salute flag)	Principal reluctant to continue imposing on nonparticipants (to proctor, help write items for needs assessment)	Tensions in school over contract negotiation, grievance action Nonparticipants resistant to external assistance, impositions on them
Bigtown	Most planning team members had flexible or light schedules Career education was the major responsibility of project coordinators Grant from state	Coordinator could meet district expectations for curriculum development through project State graduation requirement plans could be fulfilled through project Some team members wanted control over curriculum Activity-writing team paid	Many team members not interested in doing detailed planning	Coordinator's status in school/district uncertain; tension between her and staff

schools, where most teachers' schedules were full and inflexible. In the secondary schools, time was less of a problem because teachers had more planning periods they could use for project meetings, and some participants had fewer or no classroom assignments (e.g., administrators, counselors, department chairpersons). Also, arrangements to cover classes during one or two periods could be made with relative ease in secondary schools.

Time was more limited at some points in planning. For example, its availability became particularly constrained when meetings were held frequently or coincided with the busy seasons in schools (e.g., grading periods, holidays, and at the end of the school year). Chapter 3 addressed the effects of the scarcity of administrative time on field agents; this chapter highlights the scarcity of teacher time, which had the greatest effect on participation.

The lack of sufficient time to attend meetings dampened both teachers' enthusiasm toward being involved with RBS and their willingness to continue. Teachers occasionally thought the projects required too much time of them. They repeatedly urged that meeting time be reduced and came to meetings with anxieties about their classrooms. A Southend teacher expressed her feelings this way:

> There is a tremendous amount of time and paper work and
> . . . it adds up to a lot. . . . I feel as though . . . during the school
> week, there is so little time when I'm not "engaged" in teach-
> ing or in doing school-oriented work and the time when I'm at
> school when I'm not actually teaching is so precious and I have
> so many things that I have to prepare for school and then to
> take that time out to attend meetings or to fill in these
> questions or to calculate whatever. If I do that at school, then
> all of the things I should have done in school I have to do after
> school unless I have an RBS meeting till 5:00, then I have to
> take it home and do it at home and I know that teachers are
> supposed to stay up until midnight marking papers, but then
> they don't have any time to do my wash. I know it has to be a
> time consuming thing because it's so involved and that's un-
> fortunately the rules of the game, but I just felt as though
> it was a tremendous amount of work and as I said before,

maybe if we didn't have the other things that had to be done this year. . . .

Although most teachers were convinced that making classroom changes was important, they wanted to devote a limited amount of time to formal planning. Consequently, field agents and administrators occasionally decreased meeting time, carried out some planning tasks themselves or with smaller groups of teachers, and omitted or abbreviated some planning steps. However, reducing the amount of participation meant fewer opportunities to accomplish what the supporters of participation say it should: building commitment, developing local capacity, and tailoring changes to the various sites.

How administrators arranged for teachers to meet also had implications for the form and effects of participation. Several alternatives were used to free classroom teachers to attend meetings: (a) hiring substitutes, (b) asking nonparticipants to cover classes, and (c) holding meetings during "unassigned" times, for example, planning periods, lunch periods, or after school. Individual schools sometimes combined the second and third alternatives. For example, meetings at Green Hills and Neighbortown frequently lasted as much as two hours, spanning participants' class periods as well as lunch and planning periods; during the former, nonparticipants covered classes.

Hiring substitutes, sometimes viewed by teachers and field agents as the preferred alternative because it released participants for large blocks of time, required monetary resources that were not available in most schools. Only the elementary schools, where the inflexibility of teachers' schedules made the second and third alternatives especially difficult, relied on hiring substitutes. Funds for this were acquired through intermediate service agencies (two schools), district offices (one school), and related special projects (three schools). The availability of money, however, did not guarantee that substitutes would be available:

The meeting had been scheduled as an all-day session, but when we arrived, we learned that five teachers are out today, including the four project teachers (who were not "out" but

needed substitutes), and no substitutes were available. The
principal decided that the field agent should work with two
teachers this morning and the other two this afternoon. The
school has been experiencing a substitute problem all year, but
today it seemed especially serious. [A district staff member]
said that it is final exam time at the local university from which
many of the substitutes come and that many people have
colds.   (From the Patriot field notes)

Even when substitute teachers were available, their use did
not always promote teachers' enthusiasm for participating.
Many teachers felt obligated to develop more precise lesson
plans for substitutes than for themselves and spent more preparation time than usual for their classes on meeting days. Also,
some considered substitutes' instructional skills inadequate;
teachers reported they began to feel guilty about neglecting
their students. The following are illustrative, although extreme, examples.

The teacher said she is unhappy about having to have a
substitute teacher during the project meetings. Her classroom
is very well organized. Kids know what they are supposed to
do when they enter the classroom in the morning; little time is
lost during the first few hours of school. When she returns
after having a substitute it often takes the students time to get
back into that routine. She told about having a parent tell her
that once she was walking past the school and saw her daugh-
ter standing in the second story window of the teacher's
classroom. Another parent once called about a discipline
problem. . . . Both times, a substitute was replacing her. . . .
She . . . has left project meetings to look into her classroom;
she has seen many students misbehaving.   (From the Patriot
field notes)

The teacher talked a bit about the unqualified substitutes that
have been covering classes during project meetings. She described one as a "nut." The woman tells the kids she is Dracula
and threatens them with strange things. The teacher said that
one mother came into her classroom when that woman was
substituting and took her kid home. Another substitute, a
male, is an alcoholic. She said that some substitutes expect to

just sit at the desk; they don't even attempt to keep kids occupied. (From the Patriot field notes)

Such pressures occasionally led teachers to urge that meetings be held less frequently or to threaten to withdraw from projects. Consequently, field agents sometimes reduced the number of meetings or shortened activities.

In several secondary schools, nonparticipants were asked to proctor classes during project meetings. To do so, proctors either sacrificed their planning periods (in three or more schools) or, in one open-spaced building, taught two classes in adjacent spaces. This type of arrangement, naturally, imposed upon nonparticipants and caused them, according to informants, to resent the projects. Participants were aware of this resentment and became anxious about the time they spent in meetings. Furthermore, this resentment reduced the likelihood that projects could be disseminated successfully to the other teachers.

Holding meetings during participants' free time meant that the meetings were brief, two hours at most and even 40 minutes in one school. Frequently, there was even less time than scheduled because participants arrived late and/or left early. In addition, teachers simply did not like having to relinquish time they considered their own.

Incentives and Disincentives

Basically, what the above discussion says is that in situations where teacher release time was either scarce or obtained at the expense of peers, participation served not as an incentive but as a disincentive for involvement. Incentives are the perceived benefits of engaging in some behavior; disincentives are the penalties one suffers for engaging in the behavior or the rewards for not doing it (Sieber, 1981). The primary incentives in the RBS projects were improved student achievement, the receipt of favorable (or avoidance of negative) evaluations from administrators, professional contact, the opportunity to exert influence over curriculum, and escape from negative sanctions for not meeting state graduation requirements. Major disincen-

tives in the RBS projects were reduced effectiveness in performing regular teaching responsibilities, lack of expected
benefits, and aggravated or strained relations with peers. The
incentives and disincentives that influenced participation in
each school are shown in Table 5.

Incentives. A major incentive for participation was the
probability of improved student achievement. This was a substantial incentive in the basic skills schools. All but one of these
were elementary schools where basic skills instruction was a top
priority. In fact, this goal was ranked first in all of the elementary schools according to a survey conducted in the first year of
the study (see Firestone and Herriott, 1981a, for more information on the survey). In addition, several elementary schools
had long histories of low achievement test scores, and staff
reported that the schools' communities, central offices, and
state departments were demanding that the scores be improved. Student achievement in career education and citizenship education was a much less serious concern but still was an
incentive. At Green Hills, students had scored low on the
career education portion of a state-wide examination and the
district central office wanted the school to adopt the program;
therefore, people felt compelled to support it. Also, some
individual participants were particularly interested in or concerned about career or citizenship education.

Receiving favorable evaluations from administrators or
avoiding negative evaluations were other incentives for participating. In several schools, people who were asked to join
planning teams said that they did not feel free to decline. One
teacher reported that everyone in the school was expected to
take part in at least one special project and knew that declining
this one meant accepting another. Principals at Southend and
the two Smalltown schools made clear from the outset that they
thought the projects were very important. Staff found out just
how important they were when the principals included time-
on-task observations in their evaluation procedures. Consequently, teachers thought that participation would increase
their chances of being evaluated favorably. An employee at
Bigtown who was expected to develop a career education

curriculum realized that the project would help accomplish that objective. In this case, motivation went beyond simple participation to assuming leadership in order to ensure that the curriculum would be developed.

A third incentive might be called "professional contact." Team members valued the opportunities to interact with one another and with outside "experts." In several schools they reported that, aside from project meetings, they seldom interacted with one another, particularly about professional matters. They liked exchanging ideas, learning from one another, and being treated as professionals. The following interviews illustrate this:

> She said the brainstorming session [about strategies for increasing time on task] "was the most valuable to me." She said it was a "free, open atmosphere." The teachers were able to talk about what should be done in the school. She said there are not many other opportunities to talk about these sorts of things. Through the session, she learned that everyone else had the same concerns she did.   (From the Middletown field notes)

> The teacher said that being on the [planning team] was very rewarding because she likes the idea of having teachers teach other teachers. [Planning team members helped train other participants.] It seemed important to her that people responsible for the project acknowledged that teachers were capable of helping one another. She said that she has said for years that there are good people on the staff at Middletown School and that they can help one another. She feels that "we proved that this year."   (From the Middletown field notes)

In addition, participation sometimes enabled teachers and administrators to know and understand each other better and gave them an opportunity to interact with outside professionals. Project meetings were sometimes attended by employees of intermediate service agencies and state departments as well as RBS staff.

A fourth incentive that attracted participants was the opportunity to influence decisions about changes that would affect them. This was especially important to the department chairpersons on the Bigtown planning team. The chairpersons were mostly responsible for determining curricula. Although they did not express much interest in career education per se, they were keenly interested in approving or disapproving plans for incorporating career awareness activities into their respective subjects.

A fifth incentive for participation was the avoidance of negative sanctions for not meeting state requirements. While the projects were in progress, the state in which Bigtown and Oldtown were located issued graduation requirements that included career education. Schools had to report to the state how they intended to meet the requirements. The projects were readily available vehicles for developing such plans.

Disincentives. A major disincentive for participation was project interference with teaching efficiency. The time and energy spent in meetings threatened people's abilities to carry out their other duties. Some teachers reported they felt negligent when their classes were taught by substitutes. Others said they were expected to cover specific curricula and feared they would not be able to do so, particularly when participation also meant inserting new activities into an already-tight curriculum. In response to this, some people asked that project activities be scaled down; otherwise, they might have to withdraw.

A second disincentive to participants was the lack of expected benefits. This had less to do with the RBS projects than with experiences in previous projects. Many had taken part in similar previous efforts and saw few outcomes. As one field agent wrote:

> The similarity to [another project] and experience [the] school has had with [it] tend to make teachers and other adults feel that nothing will be accomplished although verbal agreement will be made. . . . Their input from past experiences, according to participants, tends to be forgotten and their work remains "paper programs." In other words, no real changes, progress, improvements have occurred or will occur. (From the Riverside field notes)

Teachers also commented that more projects were started than completed. Some people were skeptical that RBS field agents could help them. As one teacher said: "Experts have come here before and they didn't turn out to be experts; we've been led to develop stuff here that's never been used" (from the Suburban field notes). Teachers in another school suspected that RBS staff would not understand inner-city school problems well enough to be of any help.

Another disincentive was aggravated or strained relations with peers. Nonparticipants resented having to give up planning time to proctor classes while team members attended meetings. This situation became even worse when project meetings ended half-way through a class period and proctors watched planning team members leave for lunch early. Another source of irritation was that other teachers sometimes perceived a project as a "frill" and thought that team members received special favors from administrators. Furthermore, participants occasionally did not even have to go to the school because meetings were held at another location.

Tensions

A third school contextual factor that influenced participation was the existence of tensions within schools. Tensions were discussed extensively in Chapter 3; thus, they will only be noted briefly here. Tensions that influenced participation in each school are noted in Table 5. A major effect of the tensions was to inhibit the development of commitment and motivation. The tensions led to conflict, hostility, and low morale. Occasionally, meetings were disrupted because team members argued with one another. At other times, prior incidents curbed people's ability to deal with the tasks at hand. Although tensions usually remained under the surface, their existence still impeded active discussion.

MEDIATING THE INFLUENCE OF SCHOOL CONTEXT

The considerable difficulty that teacher involvement can pose for a school brings the discussion back to the premise of Chapter 3: One of the major benefits of having field agents at a site is that they can adjust the process as local events dictate.

One of the most critical adjustments field agents made in the RBS projects was to alter the nature of participation at a site so that it would not create resentment and would facilitate the development of commitment to both the process and the intended changes. These adjustments included (a) using multiple participant groups, (b) reducing the extent of participation, (c) modifying meeting arrangements, and (d) involving fewer teacher participants.

Using Multiple Groups

Nine of the 14 projects had more than one participant group. These additional groups were either subgroups of initial planning teams, expansions of teams, or entirely separate groups. They were established for different purposes and served different functions, but their effect was to disperse the demands placed on any one set of individuals, thereby rebalancing the costs and benefits scale in favor of benefits. In all, four different sets of groups were used in the RBS projects.

One set of groups was established to perform work initially expected of the original planning teams. At Neighbortown and Farmcenter subgroups worked together for brief periods of time, doing such tasks as developing goals. Because they worked more efficiently than the larger planning teams, they reduced resource requirements. A small planning group at Bigtown functioned similarly, but also helped deter resistance from planning team members who were not interested in doing the work themselves. A major portion of the project at Middletown was assigned to a second planning team, lightening the burden of the first. That substantially increased the number of participants. However, using such small groups also lessened the involvement of other participants and potentially lessened opportunities to build their commitment to implementation.

Field agents trained a second set of groups to be local leaders of the basic skills planning team. The team leaders generally met with RBS field agents before meetings to review technical materials they would help present to other members and to plan meeting agenda. In addition to leading meetings and sometimes helping arrange and conduct other activities, team leaders developed expertise in technical aspects of the projects and could help teachers with the procedures. This reduced reliance on external assistance and increased professional interaction among staff.

A third set of groups was established to do classroom-level planning—work that was not appropriate for participants who did not teach. At Green Hills and Neighbortown, these were subgroups of the planning teams. At Bigtown and Oldtown, entirely separate committees were formed. With this process adjustment, classroom-level planning was carried out by the people who would implement the plans and knew what was appropriate and feasible in their situations.

A fourth set was used to expand the projects to other portions of the schools. Several teachers at Green Hills and Neighbortown were added to the initial committee shortly before classroom-level planning began so that all major subject areas would be represented. At Middletown, a group entirely separate from the original team was formed to include people who had not participated to that point. Members implemented changes without spending as much time in meetings as initial groups. The only potential disadvantage of this was that the new participants had been less involved in the initial planning stages when the program definition and goals were established. Thus, they were expected to accept these program features without the benefit of the preliminary discussions and development activities.

Reducing the Extent of Participation

Another way to deal with the effects of scarce resources and the associated disincentives was to reduce the amount of participation. This was accomplished in two ways. First, RBS field agents, school administrators, or other employees sometimes performed tasks that were initially expected of planning teams. For example, the field agent at Green Hills often asked planning team members to react to alternatives instead of requiring them first to brainstorm them. Similarly, the principal at Southend conducted classroom observations for teachers. A Bigtown district administrator worked through most of the planning activities with the field agent and then submitted the results to the planning team for review.

Second, project procedures were sometimes abridged (discussed further in Chapter 4). This was accomplished by, for example, cutting down the number of observations in basic skills schools and postponing and eventually eliminating a survey of community resources at Green Hills and Neighbortown. Reducing the extent of participation naturally reduced the chances that intended benefits would be realized. Thus, when field agents chose this alternative, they had to weigh it against the potential consequences of maintaining teacher involvement at the current level.

Adjusting Meeting Arrangements

Meeting arrangements were sometimes altered to make it easier for participants to attend. For example, meeting times varied at Green Hills so that teachers would not always miss the same class. Meetings in some schools spanned lunch or planning periods, when teachers were not scheduled to be in class and would not have to be replaced. Sometimes meetings were postponed to reduce the pressure participants felt to perform their regular responsibilities.

Involving Fewer Teacher Participants

Participation required fewer resources when it primarily involved people who did not have classroom teaching assignments, such as administrators and their assistants, specialists, counselors, department chairpersons (who had fewer teaching assignments than other teachers), community members, and students. On most career and citizen education planning teams, teachers were outnumbered by others. However, this process adjustment had to be made with considerable care. Most of the project changes were to be made by teachers, and thus they would be the major benefactors of participation. Planning teams where teachers were in the minority could have been not only less effective in planning but also counterproductive to building a firm commitment to classroom-related changes. Such did not seem to be the case in the RBS projects, however, primarily because this adjustment was made in response to school conditions and was not an original feature of the project.

MEDIATING LOCAL CONDITIONS AND BUILDING COMMITMENT

The preceding sections of this chapter described how school context substantially influenced teachers' participation in the projects. In response, field agents adjusted the process to reduce negative influences. Many of those adjustments, however, also changed the nature and extent of participation, primarily by reducing participants' responsibilities, activities, and time. Given these modifications to the planning process, to what extent was one of the major intents of participation achieved: developing local commitment to the projects? That is, did the extensive changes in the participation process seriously hamper its effectiveness?

Qualitative data gathered in open-ended interviews do not lend themselves to quantification. However, research staff could make rough judgments about the level of commitment in most schools. These judgments were based on data concerning teachers' beliefs about the importance of making changes, their willingness to devote time and energy to planning and implementation, and expressions of ownership of the project (e.g., whether they referred to a project as the school's or RBS').

These assessments yielded three clusters of schools. The first cluster consisted of five schools that clearly showed a higher commitment than the others. All these schools were in basic skills projects. Middleburg was the only basic skills school not in this cluster. The second cluster, four schools, also showed considerable commitment, but a number of staff had mixed or negative attitudes toward the project. In this cluster were Green Hills, Neigbortown, and Oldtown—all career education schools—and Suburban, a citizen education school. Commitment was less uniform among teachers in the third cluster, although several teachers in each school were avid project supporters. This group contained one career education school (Bigtown), one basic skills school (Middleburg), and the three remaining citizen education schools.

When this ordering of school commitment to the projects is juxtaposed with the summary of important local conditions back in Table 5, it appears that negative barriers to participation in a school's context did not always produce a low commitment among participants. To be sure, the expected relationship between context and commitment did appear in some schools. At Southend the context for school improvement was mostly supportive, and commitment was clearly present; at Urban there were strong barriers to participation, and commitment was correspondingly low.

However, there were also schools where the expected relationship did not exist. Contextual conditions had strong negative influences at Patriot and Middletown—time was scarce, substitutes were unsatisfactory, and tensions existed between teachers and administrators. Yet, commitment was high. Conversely, little commitment developed at Farmcenter despite the fact that conditions seemed supportive.

There are at least two explanations for these counterintuitive findings. The first addresses the question set forth in the first paragraph of this section. Field agents deliberately intervened to mediate the influence of local conditions. Process adjustments were usually made to prevent context from seriously disrupting participation, for example, from causing teachers to withdraw or schools to discontinue projects. Field agents knew that their adjustments would change the process and perhaps reduce its effects, but they considered that less threatening than the potential consequences of strong disincentives to participate.

Second, development of commitment was influenced by other factors as well. Some projects were terminated before the effects of participation could be strongly felt. For example, RBS withdrew from Farmcenter after approximately one year (for reasons unrelated to the specific project). This action appeared to have detrimental effects on commitment even though the context at the school itself was mostly supportive.

SUMMARY

Local participation in change projects requires considerable time and energy. The extent to which people are willing and able to devote themselves to such projects is influenced by the availability of resources, the incentives and disincentives participants perceive, and school tensions that can impede productive group work. Fortunately for field agents, participation can be adjusted in several ways to reduce the influence of school contextual factors without apparently impairing the development of local commitment to the project. An especially effective way to do this is to establish multiple participant groups. Subgroups of a planning team can often carry out tasks more efficiently than the larger team and accelerate the accomplishment of specific tasks. Subgroup members can follow through on separate planning tasks or portions of a project, conduct classroom-level planning, or be trained for project leadership. Other adjustments to the planning process include reducing the extent of participation by eliminating part of the process or conducting it outside the school, for example, at an external agency. Also, meeting times can be adjusted to better fit participants' schedules. Finally, the composition of planning teams can be altered to reduce the number of participants with full-time teaching assignments.

As stated, these methods of reducing the amount of participation do not seem to lessen its beneficial effects on commitment. Nevertheless, field agents must carefully consider the potential consequences of those adjustments when deciding whether to make them. The key is to keep the balance tipped in favor of benefits over costs. Too much concentration on just the costs to participants could, in some instances also remove the benefits.

6 Change Outcomes: Implementation

An important measure of a change project's ultimate effectiveness is how widely promising new practices get implemented in a school (Miles, 1982). This, however, is easier said than done. Studies of other occupations indicate that innovative practices do not spread smoothly throughout a body of practitioners (Rogers, 1962). Diffusing innovations in organizations like schools compounds the problem. A field agent must understand not only individual idiosyncrasies, but also the quirks that make the organization unique. This chapter focuses on one dimension of school organization that determined the extent to which innovative practices spread *within* a school: school linkage. Linkage refers to the extent to which school subunits are interdependent. Essentially, the rule is that the more interdependent subunits are, the more likely change will spread beyond project participants.

This chapter first examines the concept of linkage and its relationship to the number of teachers in a school who implemented new practices. Next, it discusses planning teams and the linkages that temporarily bound them together. The major concern in this section is how these linkages contributed to widespread implementation within the teams. Third, the chapter addresses the issue of spreading change beyond the planning teams. In doing so, the spotlight is on implementation strategies that take advantage of the kinds of linkages in a school as a whole. The chapter concludes with some lessons from this journey into school linkage.

SCHOOL LINKAGES
AND THE QUANTITY OF IMPLEMENTATION

The history of thought about organizational behavior reveals a recurring fascination with slippages between intents and actions. Even before Weick (1976) popularized this focus under the rubric "loose coupling," characterizations of linkages among an organization's members and subunits richly dotted the literature (Corwin, 1981). In its simplest form, organizational linkage refers to the degree to which parts of a system are able to function independently of one another. In a loosely linked school, teachers may respond to an administrator's directives much differently from the way the administrator intended; that is, if they respond at all. In a school with closer linkages, when one staff member acts, others have to respond.

Several authors have noted that the nature of school linkages can have peculiar effects on change activities. For example, teachers who rarely have to coordinate their actions with others can easily initiate instructional changes, whereas teachers who must clear changes through appropriate channels have considerably less freedom (Weick, 1976). On the other hand, should someone in a loosely linked school decide that an innovation ought to be implemented throughout the faculty, they may encounter considerable obstacles; the mechanisms to induce and maintain new behavior in others may very well be missing (Firestone and Herriott, 1981b). Recent empirical research lends credence to the idea that widespread and systematic changes are not likely to be made in schools where few linkages exist among its members (Corbett, 1982a; Deal and Celotti, 1980; Rosenblum and Louis, 1981).

This issue is especially salient for technical assistance agents because the research overwhelmingly suggests that schools tend to have loose, rather than tight, linkages (Miles, 1981). In other words, the organization of most schools is apt to frustrate the spread of new practices, unless special steps are taken.

The first step is to understand what linkages look like; that is, to recognize characteristics that indicate the extent of a school's linkages. Weick (1976) singles out examples of loose bonds in schools, including a slow spread of influence, the absence of regulations, high teacher autonomy, low visibility of work performances to others, few efforts to coordinate activities, and few prerequisites for courses. Lortie (1969) and Deal and Nutt (1979) highlight the notion of a zoning of control over organizational decisions; Rosenblum and Louis (1981) emphasize the influence of key administrators as a connecting device and Blumberg (1980) points to shared understandings among educators about teaching and its goals as "the glue that binds" (p. 4).

This study examined how three indicators of the relative presence or absence of school linkages related to implementation. First, it looked at the amount of time teachers in departmental or grade-level meetings spent discussing issues as opposed to listening to one person make a presentation. Through such horizontal communication, teachers would more likely develop the kind of shared understandings Blumberg (1980) noted. This, in turn, could result in some joint planning of instruction. Second, the study investigated the extent to which school rules actually governed teachers' actions. Here, the focus was on the vertical linkage between formal policy and actual behavior. Third, it examined the amount of agreement among teachers about the importance of the RBS project's content area as a school goal. High agreement would indicate that teachers were at least united in their beliefs about what is important in schooling.

Data on these three indicators were collected as part of a larger survey on the organization of the 14 schools. A full report on this survey is available in Firestone and Herriott (1981b). The three indicators were measured by teachers' responses to three questionnaire items: one that asked what percentage of time in departmental or grade-level meetings (if held) was devoted to discussion; a second that asked respondents to indicate on a four-point scale how consistently the school enforced policies on the use of lesson plans and curriculum guides; and another that asked teachers to rank the importance of potential goals for their schools. The school score on the first item was the average of the percentages of discussion time; on the second, the score was the average of the percentages of teachers saying rules were "usually enforced" in the two policy areas; and on the third, the school score was the percentage of teachers who ranked goals related to the RBS project as the number one school goal.

These scores were then correlated with ratings of the quantity of implementation of classroom changes in a school. Implementation has been measured in a variety of ways in the research literature. For example, Hall and Loucks (1977) assessed the different levels of use of an innovation, ranging from nonuse to renewal. Similarly, Larsen and Werner (1981) examined types of use from "considered but rejected" to "adaptation" of an innovation. In this study the intent was to depict the spread of changes in a school. Using the fieldwork data, research staff counted the number of teachers in a school who altered their classroom behavior as a result of the RBS project. This definition of implementation most closely resembles Rosenblum and Louis's (1981) notion of the "quantity" of change. A school score on the quantity of implementation was the percentage of teachers in a school who exhibited some new behavior. Table 6 lists the number of teachers in each school, the percentage of those who made changes, and the school scores on each of the linkage measures.

If the above generalizations about linkage and implementation are accurate, where the percentage of time given to discussion is high, so should be implementation. This is primarily because discussion increases the probability that teachers will share new ideas or activities they have discovered. Obviously, for an innovation to spread in a system, information about it has to reach teachers. In addition, over time teachers likely will reexamine these ideas to see how they have been used in practice. In this way teachers receive some reinforcement for trying new activities through professional interest from others.

Such seems to be the case. The bivariate correlation between the percentage of time given to discussion in departmental meetings and the quantity of implementation was .46, using Spearman's nonparametric statistic. This correlation was significant at the .05 level.

Interestingly, the frequency with which departmental meetings were held correlated negatively with the quantity of implementation. The -.60 correlation was significant at the .01 level.

TABLE 6.   Quantity of Implementation and Measure of Linkage

School	Classroom Teachers	Teachers Making Changes	Quantity of Imple- mentation	Discus- sion	Role Enforce- ment	Goal Consensus
Patriot	18	6	33%	53%	72%	59%
Middleburg	31	8	26%	58%	73%	53%
Middletown	22	18	82%	75%	20%	70%
Southend	13	10	77%	73%	85%	65%
Smalltown Elementary	35	19	54%	69%	79%	89%
Smalltown Middle	38	8	21%	70%	69%	75%
Urban	77	0	0%	60%	52%	11%
Farmcenter	43	4	9%	59%	52%	5%
Riverside	63	2	3%	62%	49%	17%
Suburban	49	6	12%	70%	69%	0%
Green Hills	45	12	27%	71%	55%	8%
Neighbortown	49	11	22%	69%	53%	4%
Bigtown	150	10	7%	57%	64%	15%
Oldtown	141	19	13%	48%	71%	18%
Mean			27.6%	63.8%	61.6%	34.8%

This suggests that simply holding meetings is not indicative of linkages. *What is important is the nature of the interaction that goes on in the meetings.*

In addition to the horizontal bonds among individuals with similar status in a school, there can be vertical bonds between formal policy and individual behavior. When policies are consistently enforced, one would expect greater compliance with them; and when staff members generally comply with policies, policy changes can be an effective means of inducing new behavior in a school. For instance, in a school with a close linkage between curriculum guidelines and practice, any change in the curriculum should instigate new behavior by most teachers using that curriculum. In fact, such changes are one of the critical ingredients for insuring that innovations last (Glaser, 1981).

Although the projects did not actually attempt to alter formal policy, in some schools policies did change. Sometimes, when teachers perceived a new policy regarding project-related changes (regardless of whether a policy had actually been formulated), they began to pay increased attention to project emphases in their classroom behavior. One would expect policy changes to be more visible or adherence to perceived policies to occur more often in schools where rule enforcement is strict rather than slack.

The data seem to support this expectation. The correlation between the enforcement of rules about lesson plans and curriculum guides and the quantity of implementation was .43, significant at the .06 level.

The third indicator of linkage was the percentage of teachers who ranked goals related to the projects as the number one school goal. High agreement indicates that staff are linked by a common belief about the school's mission. A change effort that is in line with this mission is likely to be looked upon favorably throughout the school. Resistance toward it would be much less than in a school where there is little consensus about appropriate goals. As a result, widespread implementation is more probable in schools where agreement over goals exists.

Once again, the data imply that this type of linkage is a useful facilitator of change. The correlation was .58 and was significant at the .02 level.

Of what use to field agents is this foray into organizational linkages? By themselves these findings do little to help an agent cope with day-to-day school change efforts. An agent cannot pick only schools with interdependent tendencies as clients. Moreover, schools are not uniformly characterized by tight or loose linkages. There are, instead, pockets of tight linkages in generally loosely organized schools, and vice versa. A single strategy for implementing change is not going to produce the same outcomes in all parts of a school.

Nevertheless, these findings do have two important lessons for providing technical assistance. Lesson one is that the concept of linkage is, indeed, pertinent to successful school change. The more linkages there are, the more innovative practices will spread. If there are few existing linkages in a school, the agent can try to establish conditions under which such linkage is possible. *One way to accomplish this is to create a temporary system (Miles, 1964), such as a planning committee, as a vehicle for school improvement.* Thus, without having to revamp an entire school from the start or rejecting it as a client, the agent can establish a beachhead for implementation.

Second, the agent can identify where tighter linkages occur and use these to move implementation beyond the initial planning committee. For example, the agent may try to include on the planning committee representatives from departments that often discuss instruction; or if teachers adhere to the curriculum closely, the agent should include individuals with authority to alter the curriculum on the planning committee. In essence, the agent should first find out where linkages are and then use them to an advantage.

Of course, it is easy to give advice; more difficult to use it. The suggestions above, along with their problems and prospects, are examined more closely in the next two sections.

TEMPORARY SYSTEMS: CREATING LINKAGES TO PROMOTE CHANGE

The previous section contained some good news and some bad news for field agents. The good news was that tight linkages in a school facilitate systematic and widespread change; the bad news was that field agents will not likely find many schools that have such linkages. Even though some of the schools in this study did have tight linkages, this was only in comparison to the other schools. Certainly, no school resembled an ideal type of the tightly linked system. This means that unless some measures are taken to strengthen the bonds that tie school personnel together, the prospects for comprehensive change are dim indeed.

In lieu of undertaking a massive organizational restructuring before beginning to improve a school's instructional program, an agent can help establish a temporary system for implementing change. A temporary system consists of a group of individuals who engage in a joint task for a limited period of time (Miles, 1964). Typically, a small subset of organizational members comprise such groups. Through frequent discussions and joint tasks, this group will gradually show signs of being tightly linked, which, at least within the group, should lead to successful implementation of new practices.

Consider the differences in linkages between RBS planning groups and the schools as a whole. First, most teachers in the 14 schools had few moments to talk shop with their peers; members of the planning teams were regularly able to toss around ideas and brainstorm activities. Second, most teachers made instructional decisions about their classrooms alone; members of the planning teams usually made joint decisions that were binding for all members. Third, classroom instruction was conducted away from the eyes of peers and supervisors except for one or two days a year; participants' planning behavior was continually centerstage—providing easy access to information about skills and other resources available in the group. Finally, teachers often worked in settings where there were competing goals; planning team members were in the company of others who, by their participation, had indicated a commitment to the goals inherent in the project. All in all, the temporary systems represented by the planning teams had more opportunities for discussion, more joint responsibility for decisions, greater adherence to group procedures, and greater agreement about their priorities than existed in a school as a whole.

To be sure, temporary systems do not automatically develop closer links than permanent systems. There can be considerable variation. For example, the kinds of interpersonal interaction typically found in in-service workshops is similar to that generally found in loosely linked schools. These settings rarely provide much opportunity for discussion among participants. Individuals are usually free to act or not to act on information, and feelings are mixed about the importance of the activity. Because of these features, such workshops make no tough demands on school staff to behave in new ways and, thus, are relatively easy to arrange. Unfortunately, they seldom lead to widespread change.

On the other hand, a temporary system made up of a series of workshops on one issue is more likely to generate tighter linkages among participants. This format allows teachers to consider ideas more thoroughly as a group and grants increased time for discussions. This system may also have the added value of heightening the importance of the workshops in the eyes of participants, although in the end participants remain free to either use or not use new knowledge. Two of the RBS schools, Bigtown and Oldtown, used this kind of temporary system.

The remainder of the RBS projects used planning groups as temporary systems for implementing change. As indicated, not only did these groups meet regularly for half a year or longer and provide frequent opportunities for discussion, but they also entailed joint responsibility for decision making.

Temporary systems for school improvement can be compared along at least three dimensions: duration, extent of discussion opportunities, and degree of joint decision-making responsibility. Table 7 compares the three types of temporary systems discussed above on each of these dimensions and makes some guesses about the nature of linkages likely to result in each system and the quantity of implementation to expect.

Systems of short duration, with few chances for discussion and no shared responsibility for acting on information, will

TABLE 7.   Dimensions and Examples of Temporary Systems

DIMENSIONS OF SYSTEM CHARACTERISTICS	TEMPORARY SYSTEMS		
	In-Service	Workshop Series	Planning Committees
Duration	Short	Medium long	Long
Discussion opportunities	Nonexistent or few	Occasional	Many
Decision-making responsibilities	Individual	Individual	Joint
System linkages	None	Loose	Tight
Quantity of implementation	A few individuals will innovate	More individuals will innovate	Most individuals will innovate

probably develop few linkages among members. Systems with characteristics further along the three dimensions will tend to exhibit closer linkages. Given the relationship between linkage and implementation, it is possible to predict the spread of change throughout the temporary system. Systems resembling one-day workshops will foster few individual changes; workshop series will lead to more individual changes; and changes will be implemented by most members of planning teams.

The planning teams and workshop groups in the RBS projects fell close to the tightly linked end of the continuum. For this reason, one would expect that most project participants would have altered their behavior to be in line with project goals. The data in Table 8 support this expectation for teachers. In 12 of the 14 schools, most (if not all) participants changed their classroom behavior, at least initially.

The two schools where participants did not implement new practices do not constitute a large enough sample to generalize

TABLE 8.   Implementation Among Planning Team Teachers

School	Number of Teachers on Planning Team	Teachers Making Changes
Middleburg	8	8
Urban	4–5	0
Suburban	4	4
Riverside	3–6	2
Smalltown Middle	4	4
Smalltown Elementary	4	4
Farmcenter	5	3
Southend	7	7
Oldtown	20	19
Bigtown	10[a]	10
Neighbortown	7	6
Green Hills	6	6
Middletown	16	14
Patriot	4	4

[a]Eight of these teachers were department chairpersons who had no classroom teaching responsibilities.

about conditions that make temporary systems less effective. Nevertheless, events at these schools are informative. In both cases, planning groups never showed any signs of system characteristics. Implementation failure, therefore, was not so much the result of shortcomings in a temporary system as the inability to establish any system at all.

At Urban, the group was never able to agree on a school need the project could address. One member commented, "If you can't fix our heat or improve the food, we have no use for you [RBS]." At Riverside, staff were not always able to get release time to attend meetings. This, coupled with a deeply ingrained distrust of the motives of outside assistance agencies, made turnover from meeting to meeting so great that no two meetings had the same participants present. These two examples suggest that, in some schools, it may be difficult to establish temporary systems, particularly if project goals are secondary to more pressing needs, if necessary time resources are not available, or if previous projects have left ill will about school improvement. In such schools, field agents may have to give considerably more time to initial start-up activities in order to identify important needs, locate resources, and establish a sense of trust.

By definition, at some point a temporary system ends. This juncture is a critical event for the maintenance and spread of change. Chapter 7 focuses on maintaining changes; the next section of this chapter takes a look at how existing linkages in a school can help spread change beyond the original planning team.

BEYOND THE TEMPORARY SYSTEM: TAKING WHAT THE SCHOOL GIVES

Over the years, research on the social organization of schools has achieved greater understanding of how schools work. Two findings, in particular, are germane to this discussion. First, schools tend to be more loosely than tightly linked (Miles, 1981). This does not mean, though, that field agents can stock their arsenal of change strategies solely with whatever combats this situation. This is because of the second finding that schools do not seem to be uniformly organized, either across school levels or within school buildings. Firestone and Herriott (1982) discovered that elementary schools tend to have tighter linkages overall than do secondary schools; Wilson and Corbett (1983) found that departmental or grade-level subunits were occasionally structured in completely opposite ways than a school as a whole. The significance of this for field agents is that they must alter their approaches to implementing change as they move from level to level among schools and from subunit to subunit within schools.

To do this well, an agent must spend time sensing where couplings exist and then try to take advantage of them. The next section highlights four kinds of subunits: the social club, the professional team, the administrators' delight, and the egg crate. These differ according to the nature of their linkages as well as the strategies that can promote change in them effectively.

Type One: The Social Club

Natural diffusion as a strategy for spreading change enjoys a favorable position in the folklore of teaching. Numerous observers of school life have pointed to the faculty lounge as a more than adequate means for passing gossip, innuendo, hearsay, and knowledge among staff. Nevertheless, horizontal linkages were not uniformly strong within all subunits of a school. Subsequent interviews with teachers revealed that information and change spread faster in some subunits than in others.

The success of introducing a new idea to a core group of teachers and then waiting for it to spread naturally throughout the school depended highly on the presence of tight linkages among teachers in the various subunits. Where a subunit was linked by its instructional program or where two teachers had developed professional bonds, change readily spread; where teachers tended to work in isolation, change began and ended with the teacher who formally participated in the project.

For example, in one intermediate grade subunit at Smalltown Elementary, teachers routinely talked about instruc-

tional activities, planned together, and jointly evaluated the
activities. Symbolic of this integration of work-related tasks was
the fact that the teachers had placed their desks in a common
work area in their end of the building. Two years after the
project had ended, the teachers and administrators reported
that everyone in the subunit had implemented new instructional strategies to make better use of class time, including a
complicated arrangement of team-teaching students. The team
captain said that staff new to the team quickly adopted similar
strategies and once challenged a researcher to observe the
classrooms and pick out the teacher who had been on the team
for only five months. The captain described the team this way:
"Some teams are set-up like ours. As far as interacting goes,
there is no team like ours. Now anytime one of us is involved in
something, the others automatically know. We also had a new
person in right after Thanksgiving of this year. If you went in
now, you wouldn't be able to tell who it is."

On the other hand, this kind of work integration was totally
absent in one of the primary grade subunits in the same school.
Teachers kept their desks and professional materials in classrooms, and little discussion and no joint planning took place. In
this subunit, which had remained intact since the project
ended, only the participating teacher ever made any changes.
Comparing the two teams, this person commented: "In [the
other] team, the desks are all out in the common area so that
when the teachers sit down to work they can just easily talk to
one another. In my team, the desks are all in each other's
rooms. Overall the project might have been better if the whole
team was involved in it. In [the other one], it was shared. But in
ours, that just couldn't be done."

Informal bonds also developed among pairs of teachers in
several of the schools. This helped spread change from a
teacher in the project to one who was not. This phenomenon
was particularly apparent between two sets of teachers, one at
Southend and the other at Patriot. In both instances, the
teachers said that they so routinely shared ideas about teaching
and coordinated instruction with one another that project-
related information automatically became infused into their
conversation.

The data are full of examples of changes both beginning

and ending with planning team participants. Oldtown was typical of the six schools where changes spread to, at most, only one nonproject participant. To the extent that any classroom changes were made, they were made by project teachers. Oldtown teachers said that a major reason other teachers did not pick up the changes was the lack of opportunity for teachers to talk with one another. One cause of this was a split schedule in which some teachers and students came to and left school early while others came and left later. The consequence was that there was only a very short time each day when every teacher in a department was physically present at school. Thus, few meetings or even informal conversations were possible. With no way to link teachers with one another, it was almost assured that information about the projects and new practices would remain solely with original participants.

These findings fly in the face of popular arguments that teacher-to-teacher communication is rapid and efficient. That impression may hold for some of the teachers some of the time, but it was not typical for most teachers in this study. The results of using a core committee of innovators to instigate change naturally throughout a faculty were uneven at best. Field agents can push the process along, however, by finding out where tight horizontal linkages do occur and inviting at least one of the teachers in the subunit to join a planning team. In fact, involving more than one member of such a subunit may be an inefficient use of planning resources because release time or compensation is being provided to someone who, in all likelihood, would receive the information anyway.

Type Two: The Professional Team

Fieldwork uncovered a department at Neighbortown, two at Green Hills, and one at Suburban where the horizontal linkages had a slightly different character than the "social clubs." To be sure, teachers met and talked with one another about instruction. However, they also reached decisions about guidelines for instruction in particular courses that the entire group was expected to follow. Had these curriculum decisions been made by administrators, the subunits would have exhibited both tight horizontal and tight vertical linkages. In the professional teams, however, it was the teachers who had reached such agreements.

There was a general pattern by which change spread in these subunits. First, an innovative practice took hold as a promising idea among grade-level or department members, and then it was incorporated into the group's operating routine. In working with such subunits, the field agent's strategic problem was not how to spread change; the group's own communication and operating mechanisms took care of that. The problem was selling the group, not just an individual, on the idea in the first place.

The situation was different from that of the social club where the goal was to recruit one teacher who was in touch with and well respected by other teachers and then to let that person spread the new practice throughout the group. In the professional team not only were members' work activities integrated, but they were also bound by established procedures. Individual teachers were not usually free to implement new practices without the advice and consent of the total subunit. To do so would be to treat cavalierly a curriculum already endorsed by the group.

The social studies department at Neighbortown was typical of the professional subunits. The departmental chairperson, a planning team member, resisted making any but the most superficial changes during the RBS pilot test. Although at first field agents said that they questioned this individual's commitment to the project, they soon realized that the root of the problem was not the chairperson's own reticence but the organizational nature of the subunit. Each teacher in the department taught according to a set curriculum developed by the group. Anything more than a cosmetic change in practice encroached on this shared commitment. The only way to modify the curriculum was for a teacher to develop a proposal and present it to the other members. They then rejected or accepted it as binding for the entire department. Referring to how the group handled a new idea, the chairperson said: "We'll have to evaluate how to modify it to get what we're after. We'll have our workshop this summer and in it we'll be taking a look at what we can plug into the next school year."

Once this problem was brought into light, the field agent's task became to convince the subunit to alter its curriculum. In this case, the teacher finally requested that the field agent meet with the department and explain the rationale for making the proposed changes. The teacher had done so informally but felt the project would get the best hearing if the field agent became involved. The group subsequently acknowledged the project's objectives as valuable, incorporated some of them into its priorities, designed some initial changes, and established an agenda to tackle others. That the entire department was now involved in career education was apparent to other project teachers. As one said, "they are very structured . . . that's why it's gone more there." In the end, this one meeting with a field agent accomplished more in terms of promoting innovation in the department than had several months of nudging the individual teacher.

This example amply illustrates that individual resistance to change can be as much the result of subunit constraints as individual predilections. Resolving the problem may require meeting with an entire subunit and actually selling them on the idea. The bright side of this situation, though, is that because such department or grade-level subunits have established means for altering curricula, the problem of promoting implementation takes care of itself.

Type Three: The Administrators' Delight

Field agents may come across subunits—or in the case of Southend Elementary, an entire school—where most of the bonds are vertical; that is, teachers' actions are bound, or are at least easily influenced, by administrative behavior or policies from higher levels. In fact, in this study, vertical linkages were more frequent than horizontal ones. Three kinds of vertical linkages were taken advantage of in the projects to promote implementation: (1) between performance evaluations and teacher behavior, (2) between curriculum guidelines and teacher behavior; and (3) between state mandates and school behavior.

Evaluations as a Linkage.   Principals at Smalltown Elementary, Smalltown Middle, and Southend changed evaluation
procedures to promote implementation effectively. What they
did was simply to include project-related classroom changes on
their checklist of teacher behaviors to observe. Although field
agents expressed concern that teachers might react negatively
to this, such was not the case. Instead, the evaluations indicated
to teachers that the principal thought the changes were important enough to assess whether they were actually being implemented. The effect was that all teachers became accountable
for achieving project-related goals. Interestingly, teachers in
some schools where principals avoided this use of evaluations
indicated that without administrative mandates there was little
to induce some teachers to change. As one Neighbortown
teacher said, "You need that little push. . . . [Without it] I stuck
with what is comfortable to me."

At Southend, the effect of this practice was that almost
every teacher made project-related changes, with the exception
of the physical education, art, and music teachers. At the other
two schools, vertical linkages were stronger with only some of
the subunits. For example, the middle school administrator was
a former English teacher and reported feeling more credible as
a supervisor of that department. As a result, the person had
few qualms about suggesting new practices for the teachers and
integrating them into subsequent observations. The English
teachers reported that these actions were welcomed. Although
there was not direct evidence available that suggested other
departments would have balked at these changes, the administrator behaved as if this were so and made no attempt to share
project-related matters with them.

Curriculum Guides as a Linkage.   Occasionally, teachers were
bound to curriculum guidelines established by individuals
rather than the entire subunit. In these instances, the most
effective way to spur change beyond the planning team was to
alter the guidelines. To do this, the field agent had to be sure to
involve key decision makers in planning. In the professional
teams, teachers made most of the curriculum decisions, and so
the entire department had to have a hand in making revisions.

In several departments at Green Hills and Bigtown, the chairperson was the key decision maker. Thus, the inclusion of these individuals in the planning process was critical. In fact, implementation did not really reach very far at Green Hills until the principal put department chairpersons in charge of designing new practices. In still other schools, such as Patriot and Southend, curricular decisions were made at the district level. In these schools, then, central office administrators were crucial project participants because they were the only ones with the authority to instigate changes.

State Mandates as a Linkage. In every school, project participants could point to a formal state goal verifying that the project was addressing critical educational priorities in the region. However, direct state education agency involvement was rarely sought or even felt. The only exceptions were in five schools where the state made money available or issued a regulation governing school responsibilities for instruction in the project-related area. In cases where the schools wrote successful proposals to obtain funds for project activities, the additional money gave a big boost to implementation primarily because the project could continue at full speed in spite of local funding problems.

State regulations, such as graduation requirements, had more direct effects on implementation. For example, at Oldtown, project-related classroom changes were a clear means of meeting one of the requirements. The district decided that the approach was appropriate for all faculty, and so, urged that the changes be made throughout the school. Although the study ended before the extent of the spread of the change could be determined, the mandate at least gave the project a boost in attention. As the project coordinator said: "Essentially there was bad timing for the project in the sense that we didn't have the energy to devote to the project that we should have. However, it was good timing in that the state now says it will make career education a law."

Incorporating Vertical Linkages Into a Strategy. Given that these three types of vertical linkages can advance implementation in some schools at some times, how can the field agent determine which one to use where? The first step is to check a school's evaluation system. If evaluation is frequent and most teachers in a subunit say it is important, then encouraging modifications that complement the innovation can be useful.

Second, if such vertical linkage does not exist or there is a strong philosophical bias against what could be termed a "heavy-handed" approach, the field agent would be wise to assess the relationship between the formal curriculum and teacher behavior. Other writers have termed this kind of assessment as "curriculum-mapping" (English, 1978). Still, one should keep in mind that the relationships that characterize a school as a whole will not necessarily characterize relationships in each subunit. Where the curriculum does seem to be binding on instructional behavior, including key curriculum decision makers in planning discussions could expedite implementation immensely. These decision makers might be an entire department, a chairperson, or an administrator, depending upon how and by whom curricula are determined.

Third, the field agent should do a little information gathering around SEAs to find out what is coming down the pike. There may be a logical tie-in between a change project and either funding opportunities or forthcoming state requirements that can provide a boost to implementation. In fact, Brickell (1980) argues that the most effective school improvement weapon is "a stinging mandate followed by a powerful technical assist" (p. 207). Although the sequence of the one-two punch may be reversed as happened at Oldtown, the policy initiative can still give added impetus to a project.

Type Four: The Egg Crate

It is conceivable and probable that a field agent may encounter a school where most subunits have no significant linkages of any kind. Research suggests this is the modal situation in most schools (Miles, 1981); and it is clear from the above discussion where only 10 to 15 subunits with some kind of tight linkages were found that the schools in this study were, for the most part, loosely linked. Indeed, most school subunits resembled egg crates. That is, teachers were in close proximity to one another, but their work activities rarely touched. Numerous teacher comments described this situation: "There's no informal chit-chat. Schools can be very lonely places" (elementary teacher in a school with 13 classroom teachers). "Once I didn't see her for a week and a half. I thought she was sick. She said no, I've been in every day" (elementary teacher). "The teachers write their own curriculum . . . as opposed to teachers sitting down and doing it together" (high school teacher). Such statements reinforce Lortie's (1975) depiction of teaching as an isolated profession. The data contained no instances of change having spread among the teachers in this type of subunit.

Nevertheless, several field agents promoted implementation by establishing a temporary system that had tighter linkages than existed in the egg crate subunits. As stated earlier in the chapter, a temporary system is comprised of a subgroup of a school's staff that meets for a special purpose for a limited duration (Miles, 1964)—in effect creating another subunit, temporarily put in place to facilitate change. The original planning committees in this study were good examples, and Table 8 is a testimony to their effectiveness. Tight linkages in these groups were reflected in frequent discussions among members, shared decision making, and common commitments to project goals. To move changes beyond the initial committees, field agents in three schools extended the concept of the temporary system to encompass more staff members.

One strategy to spread change was to expand membership in the temporary system gradually until every teacher was included. To an extent, field agents embarked on this approach at Neighbortown and Green Hills. In both schools, new members were added to the planning team when it came time to actually design new classroom practices. These additional teachers eventually implemented changes to a similar extent as did original members. However, no more expansion took place because both field agents and participants said that they saw problems with repeated iterations of this process. Primary among these was the need to recapitulate and, occasionally, renegotiate decisions already made. Such backtracking helped build commitment among new members but caused frustration among the original ones and increased the time span of the project. Field agents said that these trade-offs reduced the prospects of the procedure's success.

The Middletown field agent took a slightly different tack. There, class schedules were reworked so that all the teachers in each grade would have a common planning period at least four days a week. Each grade was represented on the planning team, and these representatives, in turn, became the "field agents" for the rest of the teachers in that grade. The intent at Middletown, then, was not so much to increase the size of one temporary system but to create five or six new systems. This effort met with somewhat mixed results. The reason, once again, had less to do with the temporary system's effectiveness than with getting it established. In this instance, teachers were not in the habit of using their planning periods in this way. When administrators began to take a less proactive part in seeing to it that meetings were held, the frequency of the meetings dropped considerably.

Extending the temporary system, then, was a potentially effective strategy where egg crate subunits predominated but with some caveats. Enlarging the original system seemed to become cumbersome rather quickly. Creating several new systems with original planning team members as leaders appeared more viable. The success of this method, though, required careful attention to scheduling and sufficient administrative impetus to keep the system intact long enough to begin to exhibit the necessary system linkages for widespread implementation to result.

SUMMARY

This chapter has demonstrated the importance of horizontal and vertical school linkages in implementing change. The data echo the findings of other research that indicate implementation is more widespread in schools where there are tighter linkages. The critical lesson for field agents is that they must fit implementation strategies with the kinds of linkages available in a school. Where horizontal linkages are tight, the agent's major task is to sell the innovation to individuals in a highly integrated subunit or to an entire subunit if it also closely adheres to the curriculum. Where vertical linkages are tight, the object should be to alter policies and procedures governing instructional behavior. This requires identifying key decision makers and including them in planning. Finally, where few linkages of any kind exist, the most effective strategy will likely be to extend the temporary system, either by expanding the original planning group or using individuals on the original group to form additional groups.

7

Change Outcomes: Continuation

What happens to changes in a school's instructional program once they are implemented? Are they readily retained? Or, are they casually discarded once the attention of district curriculum coordinators and building administrators shifts elsewhere? And more importantly, what can field agents do to enhance the probability that the changes they promote will last? Hunting for answers in the literature on educational change is likely to be disheartening. Although schools have been frequently criticized for their hypochondriacal tendency to seize a highly touted remedy only to replace it with the next miracle cure that comes along, few studies have systematically examined the persistence of new practices in schools.

Attention in this chapter turns to the issue of the continuation of change. The discussion illuminates some of the school-related factors that promote or hinder the extent to which an innovation is maintained beyond its initial period of implementation. The central theme is that once formal school improvement activities end, so will most of the new practices unless (1) a school is organized so that incentives and encouragement continue to flow to those making changes or (2) corresponding changes are made in the rules and guidelines governing instructional behavior.

The first two sections of the chapter discuss the concept of continuation and the research literature on the durability of changes. Next, findings related to what happened in the

112

schools are presented. Finally, the chapter draws implications for field agents from these findings.

The tone of this chapter is somewhat different from the previous four. In those chapters field agents were frequent and active participants in the change process. Thus, their behavior was constantly in the spotlight. This chapter examines what happened to changes *after* field agents withdrew from the schools. For this reason, much of the discussion focuses solely on the school. However, the role of field agents once again will be highlighted at the end of the chapter to point out how they can contribute to lasting change.

THE CONCEPT OF CONTINUATION

Researchers often divide the change process into conceptually distinct stages that often overlap in practice. For example, Hage and Aiken (1970) note four: (1) evaluation, or a period of assessing organizational needs; (2) initiation, which denotes the beginning adjustments an organization must make to accept a new program; (3) implementation, or the period during which the new program is tried out; and (4) routinization, or the stabilization of the new program as part of permanent practice. This last stage has been accorded several labels. Some researchers call it "incorporation" (Berman and McLaughlin, 1976); others refer to it as "continuation" (Rosenblum and Louis, 1981). Because the latter term connotes the idea that change can endure as the result of either intentional efforts or simple inertia, *continuation* is used throughout this chapter. The term is treated analogously to the way implementation was in Chapter 6; concern is specifically focused on the number of teachers in a school who maintained changes.

Perhaps the most useful point to separate implementation from continuation is when special external resources allocated specifically to the change effort are removed. This is much like when a patient is taken off a life support system and must maintain critical functions independently of special assistance. Berman and McLaughlin (1977) and Rosenblum and Louis (1981) both discovered a drop in the amount of change when federal funds were withdrawn from government-sponsored improvement projects. Thus, the removal of outside support seems to be a particularly traumatic event for maintaining new practices.

Miles (1964) provides another way to view this juncture in the life of a change project. He labels special projects involving a subset of organizational members as "temporary systems." As discussed in the previous chapter, project participants constitute a collectivity of people who (1) are called together for a special purpose; (2) are expected to disband when either their objectives have been attained, their allotted time is up, or their meeting is over; and (3) through the pursuit of a joint task, take on the characteristics of group life. The disbanding of a temporary system to promote change, then, can be thought of as an indicator of a shift in organizational concern from getting new practices started to seeing to it that they are continued as routine operation.

ORGANIZATIONAL EVENTS AFFECTING CONTINUATION

What happens to change when the system supporting it is on its own? Rosenblum and Louis (1981) found that in school districts where implementation went well, so did continuation. While they noted a drop in the amount of change when federal assistance ended, schools that implemented more than others also continued more (although there seemed to be a reduction in the disparity among schools over time).

However, other research on organizations suggests that this close link between implementation and continuation is by no means assured. Hage and Aiken (1970) and Yin, Quick, Bateman, and Marks (1978) discovered that special attention had to be paid to incorporating changes into the daily operational routine to insure that they lasted. For example, new practices had to be codified into rules governing action, be included in training activities for newcomers, successfully survive budget reviews, and outlast the tenure of the individuals who were intimately involved in planning the innovation. Additionally, Berman and McLaughlin (1976) found that if these new practices actually replaced existing ones, they were more likely to continue. The prospects for "add on" activities were lower. The lack of such routinizing events reduced the prospects of change persisting.

Glaser (1981) acknowledges similar means for facilitating change durability and discusses several others related to interpersonal interaction within an organization. In particular, he says that opportunities for staff to discuss changes once implemented, to provide feedback to one another on the success of certain changes, and to receive continual reinforcement for using new practices have all been shown to facilitate lasting change. Findings from a major study of school improvement conducted by the NETWORK support both views about critical events that promote continuation—that social interaction about new practices tends to keep them in place as does incorporating the changes into rules and procedures (Crandall et al., 1982).

Thus, research shows that two categories of postimplementation organizational events can influence the extent to which new practices are continued over time: (1) the provision of opportunities for discussions about and reinforcement for continuing new practices and (2) the incorporation of the innovation into operating procedures. Added to these, there is a third category: assessments of the effectiveness of changes. As Rogers (1962) observes, not all changes should be continued. Presumably, some changes will prove useful in assisting attainment of desired goals and others will not. Less useful changes will likely be discarded.

Significantly, the cumulative research on implementation warns that knowing that certain critical events must take place does not insure their occurrence. In fact, one of the major lessons from the past decade is that there are powerful conditions in a school's context that can stall, stop, or speed up the change process—and often in spite of determined, intelligent, and committed individuals (Berman, 1981). Field agents must pay careful attention to school characteristics that can ease or block the occurrence of these events after implementation. It is to this issue that this chapter now turns.

CRITICAL POSTIMPLEMENTATION EVENTS
AND CONTINUATION

Changes implemented during the RBS projects were of two types: (1) individual changes staff made in how they carried out their instruction-related responsibilities, for example, new classroom activities, a different sequencing of lessons, new classroom management techniques, and new supervisory emphases; or (2) alterations in procedures or policies. This chapter addresses only the continuation of the former type of changes; the latter were not major objectives of the projects and tended to be peripheral to classroom instruction, for example, procedures for arranging bulletin boards, additions to student honor codes, or minor scheduling changes.

In 12 of the 14 schools more than a year had passed between the end of formal project activities and the continuation interviews. Of these 12, teachers in five schools had essentially maintained the classroom changes they had implemented; in six schools, the number of teachers who had continued new practices was less than the number who had implemented them; and teachers in one school had never made any changes.

In four of the 12 schools, one or more administrators also made changes in their practices. Although administrative behavior was not the focus of the projects, administrators in three schools revamped their classroom supervision to include the kinds of changes project teachers made; in the fourth school, Suburban, the administrator adopted a more democratic leadership style. It is worth noting that teachers' classroom practices were maintained in all four of these schools. No administrator made such changes in the six schools showing a decline.

To say that a decline in the number of teachers maintaining new practices occurred in a school is not to say that discontinuation was uniformly evident. An important finding of this study that will be discussed later is that subunits (departments or grade levels) could display organizational tendencies different from the school as a whole. Occasionally, these organizational differences made conditions right for a subunit to continue changes that teachers elsewhere in the school easily dropped.

Thus, to fully understand factors affecting continuation, analysis of each case had to move back and forth from the school to the subunit as the unit of focus.

This section discusses how postimplementation events affected the continuation of new classroom practices. Although the events uncovered in the schools closely approximated the three categories described earlier in this chapter, there were some qualifications. First, incorporation of the changes into rules and procedures was manifested specifically in alterations in curriculum guides. Continuation also benefitted positively when project-related changes provided the means by which existing curriculum objectives could be attained, even if the changes were not formally written into the guides. Second, social interaction was critical primarily because it served as a vehicle for offering incentives to teachers to maintain their innovative efforts. Third, effective assessments infrequently took place; and when they did, they were not designed as special evaluations of the projects.

Table 9 summarizes the data on continuation and in which sites the three events occurred. The table emphasizes the importance of the availability of incentives to innovating teachers. Out of seven schools (excluding Patriot) where teachers received continued encouragement from either administrators or teachers, five of the schools had the same number of teachers who implemented changes also continue them. The exceptions were (1) Oldtown where the administrator reported having so many additional responsibilities that postimplementation attention to career education practices, although given, was sporadic and (2) Neighbortown where incentives were available from other teachers, but only in two subunits. No school was able to maintain the same number of teachers making changes without the presence of incentives.

Changes persisted at implementation levels in only three of the six schools where new practices became incorporated into curriculum guides. However, such incorporation occurred only in a few subunits in each school; and in these subunits, continuation was maintained at implementation levels. As an additional note, a minimum competency curriculum in four schools (the two Smalltown schools, Southend, and Patriot) was di-

TABLE 9. Implementation, Continuation, and Three Postimplementation Events

School	Elapsed Time[a]	Teachers Who Changed[b]	Continuation[c]	Availability of Incentives[d]	Incorporation Into Guides	Effectiveness Assessments
Middleburg	24 months	8	Declined	None	None	None
Smalltown Elementary	24 months	19[e]	Maintained	Administrator & teachers	In 1 subunit	In 1 subunit
Smalltown Middle	24 months	8	Maintained	Administrator	None	None
Riverside	24 months	2	Declined	None	None	None
Suburban	24 months	6	Maintained	Administrator & teachers	In 1 subunit	None
Urban	24 months	0	NA	None	None	None
Farmcenter	18 months	3–5	Declined	None	None	None
Southend	12 months	10	Maintained	Administrator & teachers	None	District tests
Green Hills	12 months	12	Declined	None	In 3 subunits	None
Oldtown	12 months	19	Declined	Administrator	Some individual courses	None
Neighbortown	12 months	11	Declined	Teachers	In 1 subunit	In 1 subunit
Bigtown	12 months	10	Maintained	Administrator	In several courses	None
Middletown	In progress[f]	18	Declined	None	None	School tests
Patriot	In progress[f]	6	Maintained	Administrator & teachers	None	District tests

[a]Schools are ordered according to elapsed time from the end of meetings with the external agency to final data collection.

[b]Excludes awareness changes that appeared to be substantial but difficult to track over time.

[c]Determined by comparing number of individuals who initially implemented new practices with number who continued to use the new practices at the time of final data collection. "NA" means a rating was not applicable.

[d]If incentives were available to innovating teachers, the source is given.

[e]This number is a rough estimate. At the other schools innovating teachers were directly interviewed by informants. At this school informants estimated such a high percentage of innovators that follow-up interviews could not be conducted with everyone. Estimates ranged from "almost everyone" by the principal to 75% by an assistant principal to "about half" by teachers. Because administrators in most schools seemed to overestimate the amount of implementation, the "about half" estimate was used to arrive at a figure for the school.

[f]Results from these two schools must be considered as incomplete because they had maintained contact with the external agency. As a result, they had not actually entered the continuation phase of the projects.

rected at the same student skills that project-related changes were to improve. Thus, there was a mutual reinforcement between the project and the curriculum in these sites that is not indicated in the table. Effectiveness assessments were so infrequent that making a general statement based on the table is not warranted.

This section of the paper embellishes on these findings by examining each of the three events more closely in order of the apparent magnitude of their effect on continuation: (1) social interaction and the availability of incentives; (2) incorporation of changes into curriculum guides; and (3) assessments of effectiveness. A second theme of this section is that specific local conditions affected whether these three events for promoting continuation occurred. For example, local priorities, resource availability, and the interdependence of staff influenced the availability of incentives, such as administrative encouragement and peer interaction. Additionally, the effectiveness of modifying rules and procedures to support new practices was constrained by how tight the bonds were between operational guides and staff. The occurrence of effectiveness assessments is largely determined by the presence of one or both of the other two events. These findings are treated in more detail following discussion of the postimplementation events.

Incentives and Interaction Opportunities

The project planning committees were temporary systems. That is, they possessed organizational properties of their own and were acknowledged as having a limited duration. As noted in Chapter 6, the temporary systems operated very differently from the ways in which the schools, or permanent systems, operated. For example, instead of relying on students for most of their human contact in the harried atmosphere of the classroom, committee teachers were able to sit in relatively uninterrupted settings to discuss professional matters; instead of making decisions about a single classroom individually, they became involved in joint planning for the entire school; and instead of having few, if any, adult sources of feedback and encouragement about their teaching performances, they worked in a supportive environment in which commendations for action were frequent from peers, outside experts, and school administrators.

These planning committees were still in operation in all 14 schools when the first implementation efforts were made. As a result, teachers received a steady stream of queries about how the new activities were going, including frequent interviews from researchers. In addition, they occasionally had the opportunity to share their project experiences at in-service meetings, at special conferences arranged by the external agency, and with outsiders who had heard of the new programs.

Given all the attention teachers received for their project-related efforts, it should not be surprising that the most critical factor affecting the extent to which they maintained new classroom practices once the temporary systems dissolved was the availability of incentives, or "any prospective source of gratification" (Sieber, 1981). Because teachers typically work in isolated settings with very few available rewards (Lortie, 1975), the switch from a temporary system to the permanent one as the major arena for action can be traumatic for them—and problematic for the continuation of change. Such was the case in the schools in this study. Where either positive or negative incentives (e.g., verbal encouragement or the potential of a poor evaluation) were available to staff to maintain changes, the new practices tended to be continued; where such incentives were not available, the amount of change declined (see Table 9 once again).

There were three major potential sources of incentives: administrators, other teachers, and students. By far, the most important source for maintaining change at the school level was the building administrator (see also Corbett, 1982b). The typical teacher's interactions with the other two sources were not frequent enough to make them as effective in encouraging continued innovative behavior, except in a select few subunits where teachers did routinely discuss instruction with one another. (This is not to discount the salience of peers and students for maintaining other kinds of teacher behavior.)

Administrators as a Source of Incentives. In four of the five schools where changes were continued, there was at least one administrator in the building who exhibited a keen interest and played an active part in the projects. In fact all four also made changes in either their supervisory or leadership style, even though this behavior was not a focus of the RBS effort. In the fifth school, a district administrator whose office was located in the school building was an ardent project supporter.

At Smalltown Elementary, Smalltown Middle, and Southend, the administrators not only conveyed this interest in informal conversations with faculty and at staff meetings but also included on formal evaluations their observations about staff progress toward system goals the projects addressed. At Smalltown Middle this use of evaluations was only with the English department (which had received formal project training); in the other two schools, the administrators used the evaluations to hold all nonproject teachers accountable for progress toward the same goals as the project teachers. Nonproject teachers were provided project-related materials and, not surprisingly, used them to a considerable extent. As one Smalltown Middle administrator said, "[By using evaluations] I may have put some of them in the position where they had to do something." Thus, the administrators coupled positive incentives (recognition of the use of new practices) with negative ones (the threat of a lowered rating on evaluations for nonuse) to effectively induce a large number of project and nonproject staff to maintain the new practices. At Suburban and Bigtown, the administrators used more informal and positive incentives in support of project changes, for example, offering verbal encouragement to the teachers and being involved in teachers' discussions about project-related matters.

Postimplementation administrative incentives were noticeable by their absence at Neighbortown, Farmcenter, Middleburg, and Green Hills. The Neighbortown principal believed that teachers preferred to be left alone to do their work so "I just try to stay out of their hair." Thus, the administrator did not discuss project activities with them even while professing a strong commitment to the value of the changes. The teachers, on the other hand, noted that had someone bothered to ask them occasionally how "things were going," they likely would have continued many of the activities. One teacher stated that the new career education activities required some additional work and so, in the absence of positive incentives like recognition or a more negative incentive such as an administrative mandate, "I stuck with what was comfortable for me."

The principal at Farmcenter was defined as a "joiner" by two staff members interviewed: "In this district, we like to jump into projects but we never seem to finish them." "Our principal's a great volunteer. That's how we got into the project. He's always starting something." Continuing this habit of initiating new projects, the principal shifted staff in-service time to an entirely unrelated activity the year following implementation of the citizen education program. Two staff reported that the faculty interpreted this to mean that the former project was no longer a priority and subsequently discontinued the classroom practices devised for it. At Middleburg, the principal also replaced the RBS project with another one and, from teacher reports, with similar results.

At Green Hills, the principal who initiated the project was transferred. The new principal continued project-related planning (without RBS' assistance at the principal's insistence) but did not consult with nor involve the original planning team members. These teachers were more than a little resentful: "There has been nothing said to us. We were not involved at all. I feel like this is being thrown down my throat. . . . How does educational change take place? At [this school] it doesn't." And as another teacher said: "They just kind of dropped us cold, to be frank." Thus, the principal actually encouraged a new set of staff to be involved and paid very little attention to the original committee. Subsequently, several of these latter teachers reported a considerable drop in their enthusiasm for continuing the changes.

The question arises as to why some building administrators continued to support changes actively while others did not. Certainly the answer is a complex combination of factors, but this study found that incentives were just as important to administrators as they were to teachers. Encouragement to promote the projects was available in one form or another to six building administrators; all continued to at least engage teachers in conversations about the changes. Only one principal (Suburban's) persisted in encouraging teachers without clearly evident incentives to do so. In the remaining seven schools incentives to building administrators were much less apparent; their active involvement with teachers faded over time.

For example, the two Smalltown schools and Southend were in the same district, and the projects addressed the most pressing issue the superintendent felt the district faced: improving basic skills achievement. The superintendent backed this verbal indication of the project's importance with occasionally attending the meetings in person or sending a representative. Not coincidentally, it was the administrators in these three schools who incorporated the classroom changes into their evaluations.

Although there was an overall decline in continuation at Oldtown, periodically the administrator who coordinated the project received an external boost that enabled redirecting attention to project-related changes. For example, at one point when the administrator felt that no more time could be devoted to promoting the new practices because of a need to address more pressing issues, the state education agency announced regulations for graduation requirements in career education. Project-related changes provided the simplest way for the entire school to meet these requirements. The district directed the school to pursue this approach with all faculty, and, thus, the administrator was able to reallocate time to this work.

At both Bigtown and Patriot, the superintendents adopted the project approach for use district-wide. Of course, this development did not insure that implementation would follow; but, by the end of the study, building administrators reported that they were planning to spend much of their time supporting this initiative.

Only the Suburban administrator continued to encourage project-related changes without apparently receiving a district or state impetus to do so. However, it should be noted that this person remained in contact with staff from the external agency even after the end of formal project activities. This may have been an important source of incentives in this case.

Administrators at the other seven schools were not nearly as active in promoting teachers' maintenance of the changes after formal activities ended. However, this statement does not necessarily reflect administrative shortcomings. Instead, it highlights the relationships that existed between the building administrators and most teachers. Generally, teachers were left alone to perform their duties; the administrators' time was consumed by budgeting, scheduling, and putting out the daily fires that frequent schools. Thus, teachers and administrators rarely had opportunities to discuss instruction, unless there was an additional pressure that compelled them to do so. Such an external stimulus was not present in the schools where administrative incentives were rarely provided.

At Neighbortown, for instance, a district official actually reduced resources available to support project activities, even though the person earlier had been an active participant in formal planning. The administrator explained: "Career education is really a miniscule part of the curriculum. You have to keep it in perspective. [Because of my reduced involvement] I couldn't give people a pat on the back or when things came up I couldn't cut a couple of strings to make things go a little better. But I can't run every commitee." The official acknowledged, "We shot a mouse with an elephant gun." Subsequently, the principal adopted a wait-and-see attitude about promoting project-related efforts, and teachers reported that they assumed all this meant that administrators had lost interest in the project. At Neighbortown, therefore, the salience of the project for attaining district goals affected the allocation of resources to support change. This, in turn, affected the building administrator's efforts to encourage change—which then influenced teachers' retention of new practices.

Teachers as a Source of Incentives for Maintaining New Practices. A second potential source of encouragement was other teachers. However, field researchers' unstructured observations of faculty interactions and teacher reports indicated that the majority of teachers did not interact with one another about instruction often enough to be very effective in communicating knowledge about or providing encouragement for new practices. Moreover, 569 of 661 teachers surveyed said they felt free to call on other teachers to solve an instructional problem; yet, only 108 said they visited other teachers' classrooms. This suggests that while teachers felt they could consult with their colleagues, they rarely had the kind of intensive interactions about specific practices that Glaser (1981) says are critical to continuation.

Nevertheless, there were pockets within schools where the work of teachers was discussed frequently (see Chapter 6 for more on this). For this reason, it is more appropriate to discuss the effects of teacher incentives on continuation at the subunit level rather than for a school as a whole. In two Smalltown Elementary and Southend subunits, the teachers planned and carried out instruction interdependently rather than independently. The project teachers on these teams not only received reinforcement from the administrators but also effectively and quickly induced other teachers in the group to adopt similar changes. Knowledge about classroom practices discussed in project meetings was easily spread because the teachers on those teams discussed classroom instruction with each other several times a day.

In schools without administrative encouragement to teachers, such subunits were the only source of adult recognition for teaching accomplishments. Through the development of a group commitment to the innovative practices, support to maintain these changes was readily available. For example, at Neighbortown, the five people in the social studies department jointly planned courses, frequently taught the same courses, and evaluated the effectiveness of course activities in consultation with one another. As the principal said about this department, "they are always planning . . . they work any chance they get on in-service days." Changes in a course made by one teacher usually had implications for the others and, thus, were not made without the advice and consent of the group. Once such a change was made, it was adopted either by the entire group or by those who had similar responsibilities.

However this phenomenon was rare; out of the 14 schools, field work only uncovered 10 departments, grade levels, or teams structured in this way. In all 10 cases, new practices were continued unless they demonstrated their ineffectiveness. Generally, therefore, teachers in schools without supportive administrators suffered a considerable loss of attention at the end of formal activities. The continuation of change also suffered as a result.

Students as a Source of Incentives for Innovative Practices. Primarily because of teacher isolation, students have been shown to be particularly important sources of incentives for teachers (Lortie, 1975). However, only three or four project participants reported in interviews that students had commented specifically about particular new practices; instead students seemed to respond to more general aspects of a teacher's style than the day-to-day activities the teacher provided. The students may still have been the primary source of feedback the teacher used to determine how satisfying the occupation was, but students were not major providers of incentives for maintaining innovative practices in this study.

Altering Procedures: Curriculum Revision as a Source of Continuation

An alternative to using incentives to facilitate the continuation of new classroom practices was the revision of curriculum guides. Trying new instructional activities required teachers to rearrange their use of class time; and as a result, either existing activities had to be replaced or shoehorned into less time. Some project teachers were willing to make temporary adjustments for initial implementation but argued that they could not do so on a regular basis without complementary changes in the curriculum. In effect, old core practices had to be replaced by new ones. As Berman and McLaughlin (1976) found, if the innovative practices remained as add-on activities, they would be quickly neglected.

Incorporating new practices into curriculum guides was not unilaterally effective, however, because of differences in the bond between teachers and the curriculum. For example, at Oldtown, teachers were required to formalize in writing the activities they would use to help students meet state graduation requirements. Although several teacher informants said there was a generally blasé attitude about covering district curricula among staff members, the state requirements were more compelling because teachers would be directly accountable to carry out what they wrote. Happily for the projects, changes such as incorporating career awareness activities into regular course content offered a mechanism for meeting one portion of the requirements.

Similar commitments (although for differing reasons) to adhering to the curriculum were present in the English department at Green Hills and the social studies departments at both Neighbortown and Suburban. In each case, formal alterations in required curriculum content and instructional activities helped insure that project changes would continue. A Green Hills teacher asserted the importance of these formal changes: "There is not enough time to do everything that is expected and to do it well. . . . If you put something in, you [must] take something out." In subunits like these, without formal changes, efforts to comply with project intentions would be superficial at best. As a Neighbortown social studies teacher explained: "The way we've always functioned is to come up with the long range plan, prioritize and take care of them. To take one course and do that would not be good. We could do that and take the heat off but we would never come back to it."

The curriculum had a strong, although more indirect effect, on new practices at Patriot, Smalltown Elementary, Smalltown Middle, and Southend. At these sites, the curriculum emphasized student outcomes in basic skills, and student attainment of these objectives was closely monitored at both the school and district level. The Southend teachers, for example, prominently displayed wall charts containing the students' progress in meeting district-wide competencies. In the state where Patriot was located, public reports were issued giving a school's score on a basic skills test. Both of these practices gave an added boost to the salience of the minimum competency curriculum for the teachers. This consistent attention to basic skills also helped reinforce the use of practices intended to promote student achievement, such as those devised in the RBS projects.

Making curriculum changes had an additional advantage: It could help soften the effects of position turnover. At most schools, teachers were largely responsible for determining what occurred in individual classrooms, and there was no assurance that someone succeeding a project participant would continue the changes. For example, when the teacher who served as the project coordinator at Riverside was transferred to another school, Riverside lost its major advocate for the project. Turnover was so great at this school that only two staff members and two students could be located two years later who even recalled the names of the RBS field agents who assisted the planning committee. However, incorporating changes into curriculum guides could make a course less dependent on the individual who happened to be teaching it at a particular time. At Neighbortown, the math representative in the project prepared an outline for a course that was later taken over by another teacher in the department. This second teacher had expressed no interest in the project and yet, by following the course guide, actually made as many changes as several project participants. Similarly, new teachers in social studies at Neighbortown and on one of the teaching teams at Smalltown Elementary almost unwittingly implemented project changes as they followed curriculum guides infused with project activities.

However, a close linkage between what teachers taught and what was contained in the curriculum was the exception rather than the rule. As indicated in the above discussion, teachers in few of the 14 schools closely adhered to curriculum guidelines; and in one of these, the bond was tight only where the curriculum was reinforced by state graduation requirements. Researchers found only a few subunits in the remaining schools that demonstrated a strong commitment to enacting their particular curriculum. Thus, in most of the schools and subunits, teachers exercised greater flexibility in what they chose to teach. Moreover, even when it became apparent at Green Hills and Riverside that curriculum revisions could help promote the continuation of new practices, the people who were in the best position to instigate such revisions were not members of the planning team or, worse, were vocal critics of the project. (Later, as mentioned, a new principal at Green Hills remedied this situation, but at the expense of alienating the original planning committee members.)

Assessments of Effectiveness

The third category of critical postimplementation events identified in the literature is effectiveness assessments. In all but one of the schools (Urban), the committees were enthusiastic enough about the projects that they expressed hopes that the new practices would continue once implemented. Even in the schools that adopted and discarded projects with alarming speed, participants said they wished that somehow the RBS effort would enjoy a different fate. Ideally, the sole deterrent to this intent to continue would be when a practice had clearly demonstrated its ineffectiveness as a means to a desired goal. Yet, in the 14 schools and their constituent subunits, there were few examples of changes receiving a long enough trial to make more than a cursory assessment about their effectiveness.

The notable examples were the well-integrated subunits discussed previously. For example, at Smalltown Elementary, teachers in one team used student performance on teacher-made tests to determine that new instructional strategies had been effective. One of the teachers explained: "We have taken larger groups to teach skills to. . . . Where one teacher would teach large group instruction and another would handle enrichment or relearning activites. We have then tested the students and looked at the results and have seen a continuous increase in learning." When asked about the prospects for a new practice continuing in the social studies department at Neighbortown, the chairperson replied that the practice would be continued for the remainder of the year, at which time its fate would be jointly determined by the group: "We'll have to evaluate how to modify it to get what we're after. We'll have our workshop this summer and in it we'll be taking a look on what we can plug in to the next school year. . . . We're not going to give up on it."

There were two instances in which individual teachers made assessments of effectiveness that affected continuation. A teacher at Neighbortown and several teachers at Patriot relied on overt student behavior as a measure of effectiveness. In the former instance, the teacher maintained a practice that she intended to drop; in the latter incident, the teachers discarded a practice they were inclined to maintain.

In Patriot's and Southend's districts, test data and informal perceptions of administrators indicated that student achievement was improving. The districts credited the projects as being responsible for the increase, and, thus, the administrators continued to encourage the innovative efforts. This kind of assessment affected retention of specific new practices more indirectly than did teacher assessments, primarily by directing building administrator attention to project-related changes.

Fieldwork did not reveal other assessments that were made. Either projects simply came and went too frequently for objective (and most subjective measures) of school improvement to be attributable to any specific intervention, or objective data were so far removed from the occurrence of specific practices that effectiveness could not be clearly determined. On the whole, then, potentially beneficial practices occasionally suffered the same fate as less useful practices (and vice versa), unless alternative sources of incentives were available or new practices had been incorporated into curriculum guidelines.

Critical Events and School Contextual Conditions

The previous section points to three postimplementation events that had direct effects on whether or not teachers maintained new classroom practices. Yet, it is not enough to know that the above events are necessary to promote continuation; understanding the conditions under which they occur is just as imperative. Thus, it is useful to review these three postimplementation events in light of contextual conditions that supported or hampered their occurrence.

First, two conditions largely determined whether or not administrators provided incentives for teachers to maintain new practices. These were the availability of resources to support the RBS project and the nature of teacher/administrator interactions about instruction. Additionally, the availability of resources tended to increase the frequency of these interactions, thereby having both direct and indirect effects on continuation. Resource availability itself was further contingent upon the salience of project activities for meeting district goals (or for complying with state requirements).

Whether or not other teachers reinforced new practices hinged primarily on the organizational structure of subunits. Where a teacher's work was well integrated with that of others, incentives (in the form of encouragement and approval) for specific practices were generally provided; where teachers were more isolated and autonomous, such incentives were not available. Although staff turnover involving project participants reduced the availability of peer incentives, the magnitude of this loss was cushioned in subunits with close bonds among teachers.

Second, school conditions were not as important in determining whether new practices were incorporated into the curriculum as they were in determining whether such incorporation facilitated continuation. A positive effect resulted only when there was already a close linkage between teachers and the curriculum.

Third, assessments of effectiveness had a better chance of occurring in schools that had a lower adoption rate of new projects. In schools where principals were labeled as "joiners," projects came and went with such frequency that no single one was used long enough for its effectiveness to be determined. New projects had longevity when they were clearly salient means for attaining district goals.

Generally, this chapter highlights system linkage as a major factor affecting change project outcomes. Close bonds among teachers and between teachers and administrators increase the probability that incentives for new practices will be available; close bonds between formal curricula and classroom practices heighten the effectiveness of altering curricula. Thus, in the absence of deliberate intervention, new practices have the best chance of lasting in schools where such linkages are present.

WHAT TO DO ABOUT WHAT HAPPENS
WHEN THE FIELD AGENT IS GONE

As Glaser (1981) found, and as the preceding findings have shown, for changes to last long enough to become a part of everyday routine, there has to be someone in the school offering encouragement, approval, or the possibility of negative sanctions. Altering rules and procedures can be a useful tool, and demonstrating the effectiveness of a particular practice also can be compelling. But the former is successful only where rules and procedures actually govern behavior, which is infrequent in schools and their subunits. The latter is even more rare because without available incentives or complementary rules and procedures, the new practices do not last long enough to be evaluated. Thus, the provision of incentives is the postimplementation event most likely to occur.

On one hand, these findings suggest that the prospect of increasing the life span of innovative practices is dim; yet, on the other, they indicate that although promoting lasting change may be difficult, it is not impossible. How? Consider the following four recommendations:

- Maintain at least a low level of involvement beyond implementation.
- Keep the temporary system in place until formal assessments can be conducted.
- Tailor the field agent role to complement that of administrators.
- Try to get changes embodied in operating policy.

First, field agents may want to rethink the appropriate time to withdraw from a site. Because the field agent is typically the only person whose responsibilities specifically concern facilitating change, the field agent should be ready to assist the school beyond implementation. This assures that there is at least one person at a site to pat staff on the back.

Second, a field agent cannot assume that schools themselves will evaluate new practices. In fact, they most likely will not unless incentives to promote new practices are available in the interim between implementation and evaluation, primarily because the new practices to be assessed will have disappeared. To combat this, a field agent could persuade the school to keep the temporary system in operation longer, at least until assessments can occur. Not only would this allow more time to plan appropriate assessments, but also meetings themselves would become a vehicle for providing incentives and demonstrating that the project remains a school priority.

Third, by now it is clear that administrators are valuable sources of incentives for teachers implementing new practices. But, it is also clear that administrators provide incentives only when they already have a history of regularly discussing instruction with teachers or receive incentives to do so. Field agents should assess both these conditions early on to get a fix on how supportive an administrator is likely to be when formal project activities end. Depending on the results, the field agent can plan to stay on site longer, work hard to get the central office and/or community groups behind the change, or feel comfortable that new practices will continue to be supported after the agent leaves.

Finally, just as altering curricula can spread new practices throughout a faculty, they can also help maintain those practices. Of course, such changes are not unilaterally effective; they are useful only where bonds between policy and practice already exist. If schools in general resemble the 14 schools in this study, there are going to be some close linkages of this type in most of them. In these situations, then, reliance on the heroic efforts of an individual to champion change can be reduced by instituting policies that foster new practices.

8

Mapping Local Conditions Through the Life of Change Projects

The preceding pages have taken the reader on a journey through field agents' and school staffs' experiences in 14 change projects. Along the way, the intrusions (for better or worse) of local school conditions into the change process and their effects on change outcomes were singled out. In a sense, school conditions were a maze for field agents; various conditions would emerge as unexpected barriers or aids at different times. For example, early on in the projects, when field agents assisted small cadres of planners, the degree of interdependence among teachers was of little concern. Interdependence became keenly salient, however, as the focus shifted to making changes throughout a school. Conversely, antipathy between various school factions greeted field agents from the outset of planning and remained a constant companion up to implementation. But from that point on, the importance of this school condition faded.

This chapter maps the interplay between local conditions and the projects. It explicates a little more clearly the conceptual approach presented back in Figure 1 (Chapter 1) by highlighting eight local conditions as they emerged, disappeared, and reemerged over time. The first section of this chapter presents a longitudinal view of each of the conditions.

The second section addresses the implications of this view for field agents. Finally, there is a note on the uniqueness and commonalities of school change projects.

LOCAL CONDITIONS DURING THE PROJECTS

Figure 2 summarizes the impact of local conditions on various project elements. These elements correspond to the topics addressed in Chapters 3 through 7: field agent activities, sequential planning, local participation, implementation, and continuation. Moving through Figure 2 from left to right, one gets a sense of how different conditions intervened in projects over time. Field agent activities, planning, and participation are major issues typically associated with the first phase of the change process, initiation. Implementation and continuation are the second and third phases. One should keep in mind, however, that change projects cannot be so easily and clearly separated into distinct linear segments; the phases overlap and frequently are gnarled (Fullan, 1982).

Two more comments about Figure 2 are warranted. First, heavy black lines in the chart indicate points at which a condition's influence was particularly powerful. Dotted lines indicate where the condition's importance was minor *relative to other conditions*. They do not necessarily represent the absence of effects. Second, a quick glance at the figure suggests that the initiation and continuation phases were especially sensitive to local conditions, and that the implementation phase was less so. This is due, in part, to concentrating solely on how linkages affect the quantity of implementation. Additionally, many of the school conditions generally referred to as barriers to implementation actually appear and need to be resolved *during initiation*, despite Herriott and Gross' (1979) contention that many of these barriers are unknowable during planning. In this study, barriers prevented a project from reaching implementation. Once this phase was reached, few local conditions intervened. However, implementing new classroom practices covered a relatively short period of time. The issue quickly became whether to continue changes, and during this phase a complex set of local conditions reappeared.

FIGURE 2. Local Conditions' Importance Throughout the Life of the RBS Projects

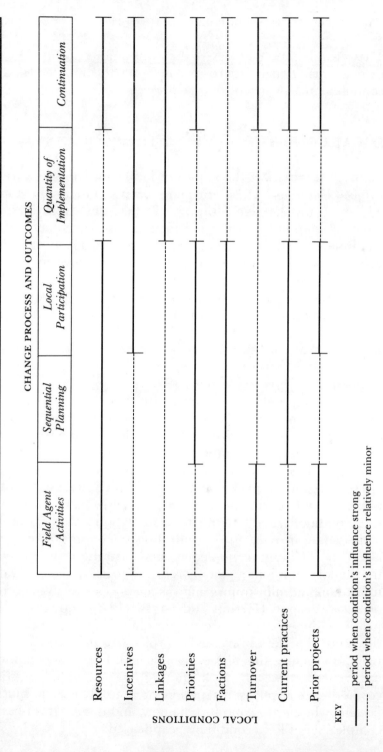

CHANGE PROCESS AND OUTCOMES

KEY

——— period when condition's influence strong

-------- period when condition's influence relatively minor

The Availability of Resources

The most critical resource, and the one in consistent need throughout the projects, was local staff time. From the outset, administrators lacked the time to be trained to lead the projects and to attend meetings. This greatly increased field agents' leadership responsibilities. Additionally, constraints on staff time in general led to (1) delays and alterations in the sequence of planning activities and (2) reductions in the amount of local participation. Later, limited time for administrators to talk with teachers about their instructional changes and to offer verbal encouragement had negative effects on the number of teachers who continued to use new practices.

Incentives and Disincentives for Innovative Behavior

Local staff behavior in the projects was influenced by a kaleidoscopic array of incentives and disincentives. Just as the childhood toy shows a different pattern with each twist, the balance of factors encouraging and discouraging participants changed as staff perceptions of priorities changed. For example, initially project meeting discussions served as incentives to participate. However, as teachers began to worry about potentially negative consequences that absences to attend meetings had on student learning, time spent in planning became a cost rather than a benefit. Interestingly, though, as projects shifted from planning tables to classrooms, verbal interaction with others once again became a highly prized reward. Participant behavior was not easily traced to any one incentive or disincentive. More often, a tug-of-war existed between incentives such as peer interaction, improved student learning, and favorable evaluations from administrators and disincentives like strained relations with nonparticipants and negative short-term effects on students caused by frequent substitutes.

School Organizational Linkages

The interdependence of staff work activities emerged as the most important influence on the number of teachers who eventually implemented new classroom practices. Where staff often talked about instruction, changes tended to spread beyond project participants. Where teachers tended to work in isolation and where principals were aloof from instructional activities, changes remained within the boundaries of the planning teams. Regular and frequent interaction also promoted continuation. No special efforts were needed to get teachers and/or administrators together; day-to-day school life provided ample opportunities to offer encouragement and conduct evaluations. An additional element of school structure bearing upon both implementation and continuation was the extent to which teachers were bound to curriculum guides. If strong bonds existed, changes were hard to initiate, but, once made, they stimulated nonparticipants to implement project-related changes and facilitated continuation among both participants and nonparticipants. As a final note, frequent interaction and adherence to curriculum guides varied as much within schools as across them.

School Priorities

When project objectives matched high-ranking school priorities, planning proceeded relatively smoothly; participants willingly devoted time and effort to activities; resources remained available after formal activities ended; and new projects rarely shoved the RBS efforts aside before their benefits could be evaluated. When project objectives ranked further down the list of school priorities, just the opposite was likely to occur. Occasionally a project's priority increased because of the serendipitous issuance of a new SEA regulation or the sudden availability of funds for improvements in its content area. Where project objectives ranked in the school was the key. All the 14 schools named these objectives as a priority. The problem was that inadequate resources prevented the schools from addressing more than their top one or two priorities at any one time.

Faculty Factions

Antipathy between teachers and administrators and among teachers played an important part in determining the course projects took before reaching implementation. Field agents occasionally found themselves having to mediate interpersonal tensions that surfaced during project activities, even though the roots of the conflict typically resided in nonproject events. Most often in such cases the field agent served as a go-between for teachers and administrators. The projects themselves also had a hand in stimulating tensions among teachers. While some participants attended planning meetings, nonparticipants often proctored their classes. To several nonparticipants this was an unnecessary infringement on their already scarce free time. Before long, they began to resent the apparent privileges being accorded to those in the projects. One effect of this was that participants expressed some reluctance to devote as much time to planning activities as they had previously.

Turnover in Key Administrative and Teacher Positions

Turnover of key participants in the projects or of superintendents did not occur frequently. But when it did occur, it produced severe problems. For field agents, the resignations of a supportive superintendent or principal was a big stumbling block. In the two cases where this happened, projects were left hanging while the field agents renegotiated continuation. Where turnover in the superintendency occurred, lengthy discussions yielded new endorsements; where the new principal took over, the school's relationship with RBS ended. Turnover among teacher participants was more frequent but generally less disruptive, unless the teacher who left also happened to be the project's main advocate. At Riverside where this happened, the teacher's leaving doomed project-related efforts.

Current Decision-Making, Instructional, and Administrative Practices

A school's instructional and administrative practices are well-ingrained. Therefore, it was not surprising that when formal project activities ended, some teachers returned to older and more familiar classroom practices. Several administrators, too, reverted to their normal patterns of rarely conversing with teachers about instruction—*in the absence of continued incentives to do otherwise.* Notable was participants' tenacity in retaining their customary ways of making classroom decisions. Teachers, in particular, relied on common, or ordinary, knowledge for determining how to instruct students. The projects, on the other hand, included long and, occasionally, tedious procedures for systematically collecting data to build a more scientific knowledge base to guide teachers' decisions. Although teachers faithfully engaged in these activities, they generally followed their more subjective intuitions when selecting which new practices were most likely to improve their classrooms.

Prior Change Projects

All the schools were familiar with change projects (some more so than others, of course). These past efforts seemed to leave a legacy that did not always facilitate RBS activities. Previous unsuccessful attempts to improve the schools soured staff about the prospects of the RBS projects, so much so that in one school staff never really agreed that the project was worth starting. Such legacies meant that field agents were met by participants skeptical about the project, its potential effectiveness, and the field agents. It was also in schools that had a history of initiating new efforts before old ones had reached fruition that RBS changes rarely received a long enough trial for their effectiveness to be determined.

Additional Influences on the Change Process

Lurking behind the scenes but occasionally sneaking in an appearance in this book were several additional factors, like characteristics of the specific innovations and the level of the schools. It is possible that several readers may have even become frustrated by the relative lack of attention given to these potentially salient explanations for the success or failure of the RBS projects.

The purpose behind this oversight was to avoid detracting from the importance of the eight conditions. Yes, the basic skills projects seemed more successful. But the explanation for this resided more in local conditions—such as the greater importance attached to basic skills as a priority at the lower levels—than in a particular characteristic of either the RBS program or elementary schools in general considered apart from specific sites. Indeed, innovation characteristics have no special meaning except in the context of the site desiring to change. And, as the sample of 14 schools illustrates, there is considerable organizational variation within a single school, not to mention within a broad designation like "elementary schools." Thus, the above eight conditions, it is argued, are basic elements for a field agent to consider. They identify potential sources of variance within and between schools and shape the meaning attached to specific features of an innovation.

IMPLICATIONS FOR FIELD AGENTS

Specific suggestions for either countering or taking advantage of local school conditions are presented at the ends of Chapters 3 through 7 and need not be repeated here. The reader should be reminded that following these suggestions will not necessarily ensure success; rather, they are offered as examples of ways to move from the research findings to practice. Capitalizing on their experience, field agents can certainly generate other action alternatives. This section takes a little more global look at field agents as they help initiate, implement, and continue change projects.

Initiation

The initiation phase of a change project draws a lot of attention—from researchers, developers, and field agents. Certainly this is justifiable. It is hard to discount the importance of getting a project off on the right foot and the compelling logic of the argument that quality planning leads to effective changes. This study provides another reason for concern about how this phase proceeds: sensitivity of project initiation to local conditions. In the 14 schools studied, all conditions except the interdependence of staff work activities affected the nature of planning, the forms of local participation, and attendant field agent activities.

For the field agent, the early part of a project is a balancing act. The agent must maximize the benefits of the project while minimizing its costs. At the outset, optimal benefits are sought through general change activities that many people consider effective: systematic planning procedures, local participation, and activities normally associated with the field agent role like finding resources, process helping, and suggesting alternative solutions to problems. These activities quickly interact with the particular mix of local conditions at a school. And just as quickly, those features intended to yield maximum benefits can become costs that dampen a local staff's willingness to participate. The field agent, then, must attempt to readjust the scales to favor benefits.

In the RBS projects, maximizing benefits entailed altering the sequence and/or requirements of planning activities and reducing demands on participants' time. This reiterates the importance of mutual adaptation as a precursor to successful change (Berman and McLaughlin, 1976). This concept, however, applies not only to the pull and push of fitting externally developed innovations to a school but also to altering the procedures by which change decisions are informed and made.

During initiation, the field agents cannot allow wrestling with alligators to blur the fact that the original objective was to drain the swamp. An eye must be kept on implementation. Despite the fact that the most critical condition affecting implementation, staff interdependence, does not seriously affect planning and participation, it must be considered when participants are originally selected. There are two important reasons. First, participants' locations within the communication and authority lines of the school affect whether nonparticipants also tend to make changes. Second, participants may start making changes before implementation is formally begun. Waiting until later in the project to worry about linkages between participants and nonparticipants would likely miss the actual beginning of the implementation phase.

Implementation

The lack of (1) horizontal linkages among teachers' work activities and (2) vertical linkages between administrators and teachers and between curriculum guides and instruction is the major obstacle to widespread implementation of new practices in schools. Many other obstacles confront a project to be sure. For example, resources must be found, the residue of previous efforts shaken off, and faculty factions finessed. But, once the issue becomes who is or is not going to change, knowing how individuals and guides for behavior interrelate can yield the best prediction. This is because such knowledge provides insights into who will know about and receive encouragement to change.

Linkages are important in both the temporary systems initially established to promote change and the overall social system of the school. Close linkages are essential to the success of whatever temporary system is used. Frequent discussions, jointly shared task responsibilities, and an agreed-to goal bind participants to one another. Thus, over time, participants develop a group, as opposed to an individual, commitment. Such a commitment should ultimately stimulate most participants to change. This phenomenon was clearly evident in the RBS projects. Linkages in temporary systems, however, vary among different methods of providing assistance to a school. They tend to be present in planning groups and absent in typical one-day in-service settings. Thus, the way in which the activities of initial participants are structured predetermines, to a great extent, the number of them likely to change.

Similarly, the presence or absence of linkages in a school as a whole substantially affects who beyond initial participants will change. If participants are in departments or grades where teachers frequently work together and/or closely adhere to curriculum guides, new practices will certainly become known and more than likely be given a trial. Of course, whether such linkages are strictly among teachers, between teachers and guides, or both implies the necessity of adopting slightly different assistance strategies. Vertical bonds between administrators and teachers are critical. Administrative mandates or attention to new practices in evaluation procedures seem not to bludgeon teachers to change so much as they indicate that an innovation is worthy, important, and favorably regarded.

There is a drawback to this line of argument. If the price for achieving widespread change is the creation of tightly organized, closely supervised institutions, then maybe the cost is too high. What are the morale consequences of severely reducing individual autonomy? This issue, in fact, may be less of a problem than it is sometimes considered to be. Tighter linkages simply mean that teachers have opportunities to discuss instruction with one another, that what sixth graders learn in one classroom is similar to what other sixth graders learn in another classroom, and that principals are aware of what constitutes state-of-the-art practice and have means to assess its prevalence. In other words, tighter linkages do not have to suffocate the staff; and they can enable a school to be structurally receptive to new knowledge and supportive of the widespread use of currently acceptable practices. Field agents will rarely be in a position to restructure a school anyway. But given their concern with altering practice, they can take advantage of existing situations that facilitate the spread and use of new knowledge.

Continuation

Continuation issues have not been heavily addressed by researchers, developers, or field agents. However, this phase encounters as complex a mix of local conditions as initiation. Scarce resources to encourage special attention to new practices, the initiation of other new projects, changing priorities, and staff turnover all endanger newly implemented changes. Without means for countering these threats, changes generally do not last long enough for their effectiveness to be determined. This goes a long way toward explaining the mixed results of educational reforms. Attention to maintaining new practices is simply dropped prematurely. Just as field agents have to navigate a hazardous course during initiation, a similarly booby-trapped path awaits implemented changes.

Field agents, then, may need to rethink the appropriate time to leave a site. The discussion in Chapter 7 suggests that schools themselves cannot easily promote continuation. Lasting classroom change is the result of continued encouragement, incorporation of changes into curriculum guides, and effectiveness assessments. For these assessments to occur, one or both of the other two mechanisms must be present; if they are not, changes are unlikely to last long enough for an evaluation to make sense. However, routine encouragement and incorporation rely on the presence of school linkages and, thus, will be effective only in those sporadic situations where close bonds exist. To overcome this, field agents probably should expand the time frame of a project to include follow-up activities after implementation.

Follow-up activities could take several forms, any of which would increase a new practice's chance of survival. First, build evaluation into formal project activities. This would facilitate peer encouragement to maintain new practices until their actual benefits can be determined. Of course, this strategy will be of most use in maintaining project participants' innovative efforts. Second, schedule some reporting activities in which participants share what they have done with others. Bring outsiders involved in similar projects to the school or work with the school to arrange opportunities for participants to speak at conferences. This strategy has the same drawback as the first in that it will only affect a limited number of innovators. Third, field agents can assist widespread continuation by working with the principal to find ways to build interaction into existing school routines. One way to do this is to identify particular times in the schedule when the principal can make a point of speaking to one or two teachers about their innovative efforts. Another way to increase interaction is to find spots in teachers' work schedules where they are free to observe and discuss one another's use of new practices. These last activities require significantly fewer resources than the first two and may, in fact, be more effective overall. The point of all of the suggestions is that field agents need to do more than assist the birth of an innovation; they must also nurture it to maturation.

A FINAL NOTE

Willard Waller (1967) once described schools as a "museum of virtue" (p. 34). Other authors since then have duly noted that despite intensive reform efforts, the classrooms of today are not very different from those of the past. Indeed, most teachers still instruct rows of restless students, chalk in hand, instilling the wisdom of the ages. This image of schools as the resilient institution encourages adherence to the belief that a school is a school is a school.

Field agents know better. Each school has its own set of challenges that must be met in ways that are uniquely appropriate for that school. This book has attempted to highlight eight local conditions that combine in different ways to give a school its individual identity. Its intent is to help field agents to understand why they can be so successful in one school and so seemingly inept in another. With such an understanding, the prospects of embarking on a new decade characterized not by the failure of reform but by its success should be immeasurably improved.

Appendices
About the Authors
References
Index

APPENDIX A
Capsule Case Histories of the Projects

There is a constant danger in reporting qualitative research. Either the author inundates the reader with detail or squeezes the life out of vibrant and exciting phenomena in order to draw generalizations. How such a tension between description and abstraction gets resolved is never satisfactory, for the author or the audience. This may particularly be the case with this study. Its central message is that field agents must take school context into account; and yet, in making the argument, the authors are able to give only glimpses of the complicated and intricate nature of these contexts. Space limitations and the reader's patience simply preclude the inclusion of twelve complete case studies. To help develop a somewhat more holistic picture of each school, this appendix contains a chronology of events at each site, highlights of salient contextual conditions, and a brief summary of the site's contribution to the study's findings. The reader may occasionally want to flip back and forth between the numerous examples that appear in the text and this appendix in order to achieve a clearer understanding of the idiosyncracies of each school.

MIDDLEBURG ELEMENTARY

Middleburg Elementary School participated in the basic skills project only during its first year, which actually was less than four months. Teachers received training in time-on-task observation procedures, conducted classroom observations, analyzed the resulting data, and discussed strategies for using time more efficiently. However, they did not reach the point of committing themselves to implementing particular changes. At the beginning of the next school year, Middleburg administrators decided to withdraw from the project. They, instead, adopted a reading program as part of an Emergency School Aid Act grant and felt they could not ask teachers to participate in both programs.

Despite all this, interviews with several teachers two years later revealed that they had become more aware of off-task behavior and of strategies for increasing time-on-task. Teachers introduced some changes similar to those made in Middletown—for example, making sure that students were never without assigned work and reducing transition time from one activity to another. As in the other basic skills sites, teachers' experiential knowledge took precedence over information generated during the decision-making process; they sometimes implemented changes they considered worthwhile rather than waiting until the designated stage. However, they might have introduced even more changes had it not been for the sequential process. After a brainstorming session at the next-to-the-last meeting, one participant said "I'm getting a lot of ideas. Can I start them tomorrow?" The field agent replied, "Well, it's not really realistic. . . . The next meeting is to plan out how you want to do a particular kind of strategy. . . . Maybe then [two weeks from now] you'll be able to work it out. . . . Then you'll want to try it." That session was held, but the intended decisions were not made before the project's end.

Two other contextual factors were also influential at Middleburg: factions and incentives. A division between teachers and administrators led teachers to question the reliability of classroom observations the administrators conducted. Also, teachers became skeptical that change would occur after the principal rejected many of the ideas they suggested (without a rationale that was acceptable to them). According to RBS field agents, Middleburg administrators had ulterior motives for participating (one hoped to springboard to a new job and the other was helping him), which disappeared after the first year. Thus, in addition to having an incentive (grant money) to adopt a different program, the administrators no longer had an incentive to continue working with RBS.

MIDDLETOWN ELEMENTARY

Middletown, the only elementary school in a 300-year-old community, has an aura that is a strange mixture of small town and inner city. Big old homes, some designated as historical landmarks, line several streets of the town. More prevalent near the school, however, are cramped row houses built close to the sidewalks. Crossing guards, cafeteria workers, and custodial staff sit comfortably in the school's only lounge and gossip about community affairs. Parents often sit in the hallway, waiting to pick up children or see the principal. Informality reigns.

Middletown eagerly adopted the basic skills innovation in the second year of the study, after Middleburg—a neighboring town—decided to withdraw. The Middletown community was concerned about low achievement test scores. Increasing the time students spent working on the basic skills made sense as a strategy for improving achievement. Besides, RBS would provide assistance without cost, and an intermediate service agency (ISA) would obtain money to pay substitutes while teachers worked on the project. Despite this late beginning, Middletown formally adopted the innovation more extensively than any school in the study. With the exception of the kindergarten teachers and most specialists, every teacher received training.

During the first year, ten teachers attended all-day meetings every several weeks. Sitting around a large table in the adjoining district school board room, teachers learned how to collect time-on-task data, analyzed the data, brainstormed ideas for improving students' use of time, and eventually decided what strategies to use. Even before reaching this stage, teachers began to change their classroom management strategies, especially after watching videotapes of classrooms in which students wasted time waiting in line to see the teacher and hearing colleagues describe techniques they used to reduce management time. Teachers worked together productively during meetings, although two types of frustrations frequently surfaced. First, teachers arrived feeling hassled. Sometimes they had learned about the meeting only a few minutes before from the substitutes who had arrived to take over their classes; at other times, they felt guilty about skipping out on their teaching responsibilities and perhaps shortchanging students. Second, the principal was often called from meetings to handle emergencies. Teachers regretted this because the project provided a rare opportunity to discuss academic concerns with the administration and because some changes could not be made without the principal's support.

The next year, these teachers worked in teams—with only limited assistance from RBS and ISA field agents—to train all other Middletown teachers in time-on-task procedures. At the same time, a separate group of seven teachers worked on improving the correspondence among content included in the curriculum, actually taught, and assessed on achievement tests. These two ventures were less successful than those of the first year. Project meetings and other activities were repeatedly postponed and sometimes never rescheduled. Teachers felt that their earlier skepticism about the project and hesitancy to commit themselves to it were justified. Indeed, to them it appeared that the principal had again adopted an innovation only to drop it after an initial burst of enthusiasm.

As the above suggests, Middletown illustrated several of the findings reported in the text: the importance of principal support to successful planning for school change and to subsequent dissemination within the school; the costs of extensive teacher participation, even when money for substitutes is available; the sometimes greater influence of intuitive understandings over the results of careful sequential planning; and the dampening effects of skepticism teachers develop as a result of previous innovations that were not followed through to completion.

PATRIOT ELEMENTARY

Extremely low achievement levels prompted officials in this urban district to agree to work with RBS in basic skills. During the first year of the project, participants learned the time-on-task procedures, collected data, and identified school-wide scheduling changes to introduce at the beginning of the following school year. For example, classroom and special education pull-out schedules were coordinated to eliminate repeated disruptions. Also, special classes such as music and art were rescheduled into fewer but longer periods rather than more frequent and shorter ones.

Two major problems became apparent relatively early in the project and continued to plague it throughout. First, tensions between teachers and administrators required the field agent to mollify teachers and to adjust the process to avoid tension-producing situations. Problems manifested themselves, for example, when the principal chastised teachers for being late to project meetings because they had helped substitutes get their classes started and when teachers objected to having administrators conduct classroom time-on-task observations. Second, although the district provided money for hiring substitutes during RBS meetings, they were not always available, and teachers considered some of the substitutes incompetent.

The group repeated the time-on-task activities the following year, this time using revised materials. The teachers decided to introduce classroom changes they thought would improve discipline. They considered this the school's major problem and attributed delays in making a smooth transition from one activity to another to it. Although this assumption contradicted the observational data, the teachers pressed on with their solutions. Factions between teachers and administrators continued to disrupt project meetings, and teachers were still not comfortable with the caliber of substitutes.

During the third year, participants focused primarily on the match among the content in the curriculum actually taught to students and included on achievement tests. This effort was similar to a new district initiative, and teachers' project work helped them meet the district requirements. In addition, teachers wanted to ensure that they covered concepts that would be

tested. This incentive helped rekindle teachers' interest in the
project. Partially due to personnel changes in the central office
and intermediate service agency, administrators participated
much less during the third year; consequently, tensions declined. Substitute problems continued, however, and required
field agents to make last-minute changes, such as reducing an
all-day meeting for four teachers to two half-day meetings for
two teachers each and providing time for teachers to check on
their classrooms during breaks.

Events at Patriot were influenced by several contextual
factors. The lack of resources—in this instance, the availability
and quality of substitute teachers—sometimes reduced meeting
time and increased teachers' anxieties about their students.
Factions between teachers and administrators created tensions
that disrupted meetings and required field agents to adjust
their behavior. Teachers' beliefs that lack of discipline was the
school's most serious problem led them to introduce behavior
modification strategies rather than procedural changes to reduce transition time, as suggested by the observation data.

SMALLTOWN ELEMENTARY

At Smalltown, a little planning went a long way. The school
participated in the RBS project for just the first year, and yet
more than half of its 35 teachers eventually made changes to
improve time-on-task. More stunning, perhaps, is the fact that
of the seven planning team members (four teachers, a guidance
counselor, an assistant principal, and the principal), only four
were still at the school by the time the third-year interviews
were scheduled.

The year of planning was conducted in conjunction with
two other schools from the same district—Southend and
Smalltown Middle. The three teams met together for the first
part of the year and individually for the second part. The
assistant principal (who subsequently moved on to another
school) was a key participant. He was the only administrator
who actually led a meeting from start to finish, including
making presentations about complicated data collection issues.

This person also began to incorporate time-on-task observations into the evaluation procedures for all teachers.

At the end of the first year, the district's superintendent had additional staff development ideas for the school, and, thus, Smalltown no longer worked formally with RBS. Nevertheless, field agents continued to stop in to see how the teachers were doing, and the administrators occasionally called RBS staff to answer questions. As mentioned, at the end of the year, the assistant principal left (to be replaced by the guidance counselor), as did two of the teachers.

Yet the changes remained intact. This site is instructive because it highlighted the powerful boost existing structural arrangements could give to implementation. One of the project teachers was in an inter-grade team that worked together closely. Very quickly, all members learned of the RBS project and began improving time-on-task. Moreover, the administrators reinforced the project by incorporating time-on-task into evaluations. These two factors seemed to spread the changes far beyond what might have been expected given the relatively small amount of resources that were initially devoted to the project.

SOUTHEND ELEMENTARY

Unlike Smalltown Elementary, Southend formally participated in the basic skills project for two years. Efforts to address this topic were at the core of Southend's instructional program. In fact, the district intentionally established Southend for the purpose of teaching the basic skills. Parents had the choice of sending their children to the tightly structured, closely disciplined Southend or to the more open, individualized instruction at Smalltown.

The first year followed the pattern described above at Smalltown. Originally teachers from the three schools in the district met together to be trained in observation and data analysis procedures. As the project moved to determining strategies for improving time-on-task, each school's team worked separately.

The second year revealed two important tensions between RBS' approach and local constraints. First, as the teachers once again began to work through the time-on-task aspect of the project (with revised materials), the RBS field agent tried to get the principal to assume more meeting leadership. Invariably, some unforeseen event would prevent the administrator from doing so. Sometimes the field agent would spend additional energy preparing the principal to direct an activity only to discover on the meeting day that the principal had to be elsewhere; at other times, the principal was present at the session but had been unable to be briefed ahead of time. Second, several other projects demanded teachers' attention. They were learning a new reading series, participating in a university-developed project, and continually facing the task of tracking student movement through the district's minimum competencies. Their complaints about too much to do finally led the principal to request that the RBS activities slow down. The tone of the request implied that the project might have to stop entirely if the teachers' time constraints could not be accommodated. The field agent responded to both tensions by assuming more leadership and reducing the demands of the process.

The above does not mean that Southend staff looked disfavorably on the project. To the contrary, during interviews one year after the project ended staff members gave the basic skills effort partial credit for a dramatic improvement in student achievement test scores; the principal continually used superlatives to describe the project and had incorporated time-on-task into evaluation procedures; teachers (participants and nonparticipants) reported making project-related changes. Moreover, throughout the difficulties about time and leadership, relations between field agents and Southend staff remained comfortable and friendly. The project had simply demanded too much at the wrong time.

Events at this site clearly demonstrated how teacher involvement could shift from being a positive influence on local commitment to an innovation to being a negative one, depending upon the costs. The site also yielded important insights into the administrator's role during the change process. Time constraints made intensive participation difficult, but providing informal encouragement and using regular evaluation conferences to discuss project-related ideas fit more easily into the principal's regular routine—and were very effective for stimulating nonparticipants to change and for helping the changes to last.

FARMCENTER JUNIOR HIGH

Unlike two of the other citizen education sites, the project in this school lasted two years. The first year RBS field agents were extensively involved. Because Farmcenter staff were particularly motivated to address community involvement as a program objective, RBS encouraged early inclusion of representatives from local service organizations. It soon became apparent, however, that the sheer number of people attending the meetings (over 15 on the average) and the varied interests they pursued was a hindrance to efficient and effective planning. Eventually everyone agreed that it would be best for the school to develop the program by itself and, then, to contact community members to see to what extent they wanted to participate.

So, after this somewhat overwhelming beginning, the project settled down to RBS working with four or five staff members. RBS structured these meetings more than intended, but this was in response to members' concerns that they did not fully grasp what planning entailed. Indeed, for much of the year, the committee teachers shared few of their experiences with colleagues, primarily because "we didn't know what was going on ourselves," as one teacher said. By the end of the year, this situation had changed; the committee developed a sense of what project objectives should be and how to go about attaining them.

The principal took charge of the second year activities. RBS was phasing its involvement out but continued to be available to give advice. Essentially, planning was shifted to teachers who worked with their everyday instructional teams. The committee assigned each group the task of developing activities for one project goal; plans included bulletin boards, special awards assemblies, and classroom activities. The principal made staff development time available for this effort.

By the third year, the principal (described by one staff member as a "joiner") initiated an entirely different curriculum project. All energy and discussion were directed to this new initiative. Staff reported that this made them question the importance of the citizen education program. And although they reported a lingering awareness of the importance of community involvement, teachers' attention to the special activities faded.

Farmcenter exemplified the positive effects of administrative involvement and the negative effects of its withdrawal. Originally, the principal was able to marshall the requisite resources for planning and, through these efforts, let staff know the project was important. Later, by switching all administrative attention to a new effort, the principal communicated the opposite message about the RBS program. In fact, this may point to one drawback of the "innovative" leader. That kind of person typically is always starting something; but for change to last, the programs have to receive some finishing touches. Primary among these is persistent encouragement and recognition for those making changes.

GREEN HILLS JUNIOR HIGH

Shortly before RBS approached this school, its students performed poorly on the career education section of a statewide assessment, motivating the district to upgrade its career education offerings and welcome RBS' assistance. Working with an RBS field agent, a planning team of eight (four teachers, a guidance counselor, a community member, the principal, and the assistant superintendent for district curriculum) decided to infuse career education into subject matter curricula rather than teach it as a separate course.

The first year was devoted to identifying potential project goals and conducting a needs assessment to help prioritize them. During the second year, the planning team analyzed the needs assessment, decided which goals to address, and wrote objectives. These were included in a program document that was distributed within the school, to district administrators, and to the school board.

The next stage of the process was for teachers on the planning team to write career education activities they would infuse into their lessons. At this point, two teachers from major departments not represented on the team were added. After writing the activities, teachers piloted them in selected classes. Most were classes in which teachers thought the new activities would interfere minimally with the regular curricula—for example, two seminars, an enrichment class, and a course for low-achievers who were not expected to get through the regular curriculum. For most courses, teachers felt obligated to cover printed curricula and/or to teach all concepts included on achievement tests that would be used throughout particular departments.

At the end of the second year, the principal was transferred to a district administrative position. The new principal decided not to continue the planning team's work or RBS' involvement. However, the district still expected the school to develop and implement a new career education curriculum. Wanting to discharge that responsibility quickly, the new principal assigned the work to the faculty council. It included department chairpersons, who had extra planning time to write activities and the authority to ask teachers to implement them. Using a few activities written by the original planning team but ignoring program development decisions such as taking an infusion approach, the faculty council completed their work several months after school started. Then, as planned, all ninth grade teachers in two departments used the new activities. Planning team members were not involved in these new efforts, except for one who was a department chairman on the faculty council and another who consulted with the chairman of her department on the development of activities. Those two people were in departments that implemented career education; one other member of the former planning team continued to infuse career education into classroom activities; the other three did not.

Green Hills provided several productive insights into contextual factors. Incentives and disincentives were particularly influential. The district adopted the innovation to improve student performance on the statewide assessment; the new principal continued it, though in a radically modified version, to avoid an unfavorable evaluation from his superiors. Planning team members encountered the disincentives of criticism from their departments for failing to completely cover their curricula because they used career activities instead and resentment from colleagues who had been asked to sacrifice free periods to proctor participants' classes during meetings. The former disincentives were created by tight linkages within departments between written curricula and classroom instructional behavior. In addition to limiting implementation of the pilot activities, the proctoring arrangements caused resistance that made nonparticipants unreceptive to later dissemination efforts. Administrative turnover, of course, abruptly redirected career education efforts.

RIVERSIDE MIDDLE SCHOOL

RBS field agents faced considerable problems in the one year they spent working in this inner-city middle school. They did manage to get two building administrators to agree to be part of the planning team, but these two rarely could attend meetings because they had to cover the everyday responsibilities of the often-absent principal. The staff present at the first meetings voted to give project coordination responsibilities to a highly motivated teacher who, for several reasons, had little influence within the faculty. This greatly limited the number of teacher volunteers the project eventually attracted. A further detriment to winning participants was the resentment left over from a long history of largely unsuccessful interventions from outside agencies. An additional problem was spotty communication of school events to faculty. Staff typically were aware of meetings only shortly before they were held.

These difficulties had a substantial effect on the nature of project activities, primarily because the only people in the school who could easily and willingly respond to sudden announcements of meetings during the day were students. As much as the field agents ardently supported the notion that students were important members of a school and therefore should be on the team, thirteen and fourteen year-olds were simply not sophisticated planners. Indeed, discussions often centered on topics like the need for ice cream in the cafeteria. And as one student said, "If a student came in with an attitude, we would try to solve their problem first so the meeting would go a little better." Progress was most often achieved by individuals (usually RBS staff or the coordinator) who agreed to try to perform a particular task between meetings. Those who attended the sessions could then react to the work and alter it as needed.

Clearly, RBS field agents assumed much of the necessary project leadership. This proved to be a death knell for the program when RBS lost federal funding for citizen education. There was no one to generate any momentum, especially with the transfer of the coordinator to another school.

Riverside illustrated a number of nearly intractable barriers to change: staff resentment of outsiders, little intrastaff communication, clear faculty divisions, and few incentives to participate. Sadly, the early termination of the project allowed few glimpses of strategies that might have pointed the way out of the morass.

SMALLTOWN MIDDLE SCHOOL

The superintendent of Smalltown's district—which included Southend and Smalltown Elementary—involved this school in the first year of the RBS basic skills project. Three English teachers (out of seven in the department) and a social studies teacher were selected to participate, along with the assistant principal. Activities focused solely on improving student time-on-task.

Teams from all three schools in the district met jointly during the first part of the year. The RBS field agents led the majority of these meetings, although occasionally an administrator from one of the schools would assume this responsibility. The administrators performed more of a leadership function in the last half of the year when teachers started discussing particular changes to make. At these sessions, the teams were divided by school, and an administrator from each site ran the meeting. Field agents floated from group to group to listen in and clarify concerns.

Smalltown Middle's team leader was relatively new to administration. A former English teacher, the person reported some difficulty in wearing the mantle of leadership. She was comfortable with the English teachers because, with them, she felt she had credibility as a subject matter expert; but, overall, she was not sure others accepted her as an administrator. This general insecurity caused friction with the RBS field agents earlier in the year over how much leadership RBS would exert. The administrator was concerned that the structured opportunities for school officials to run the show were few and far between. Indeed, RBS' decision to hold meetings by school was largely the result of this person's wish to be in a position to assert more leadership.

The superintendent decided to shift the school's major staff development focus, and thus Smalltown was not officially in the project after that point. However, the assistant principal wanted to extend the time-on-task work to the remaining four English teachers. She reported she did not feel comfortable requiring teachers from other departments to participate. Several meetings were held, and the administrator called an RBS field agent in to make a presentation. The teachers reported that the work was interesting and useful. The assistant principal began to incorporate time-on-task observations into evaluation procedures, but only for the English teachers. Time-on-task activities were never conducted with other teachers.

This school primarily served as an example supportive of the argument that administrative encouragement after the end of formal project activities was critical to teachers' continuation of changes. Interviewing during what would have been the third project year indicated that the English teachers were still focusing on improving time-on-task. The social studies teacher who was an original committee member reported that no changes had ever been made in that subject area.

SUBURBAN JUNIOR HIGH

Suburban worked with the citizenship education program throughout its nearly two-year duration. Four teachers (two in social studies, one in music, and one in physical education), the principal, three community members, and two students worked with RBS field agents to develop innovation plans. While the project did not address any existing school goals, it was compatible with the interests of a conservative community and two of the teacher participants regarding student behavior such as saluting the flag. Also, the principal saw the opportunity to work with outside experts as a means to further develop his administrative skills.

During the first year, the group worked through the problem-solving process to the stage of developing a needs-assessment instrument. However, progress was slow. One inhibitor was that the group adopted a long list of goals, thereby necessitating a lengthy instrument to assess their importance for staff. Also, the principal was reluctant to accelerate activities to avoid increasing existing tensions between himself and the staff. The project imposed on nonparticipating staff who were asked to cover classes during meetings and to help develop the needs-assessment instrument by working with RBS staff on item writing.

During the second year of the project, the needs-assessment instrument was administered and the data compiled. Further work was precluded because the RBS unit that was working with Suburban lost its funding. Project participants did not reach the point of identifying and implementing school or classroom changes. However, the social studies department later wrote a new curriculum that included an emphasis on law-related issues; the chairperson and one teacher had become aware of that need through their participation in the project.

Suburban particularly illustrated the problem of introducing an innovation that requires an extensive planning process to a site where resources are not available to support the process and the project does not address high priority goals. Nevertheless, there was a positive side to Suburban activities. The social studies department experience suggested that an innovation is more likely to influence classroom practices when it becomes a formal part of the curriculum especially when that curriculum actually guides behavior.

URBAN JUNIOR HIGH

Urban began the citizen education project after a district administrator suggested that RBS work with Urban because of its ethnic composition. The principal expressed concern that the school was desegregated but not integrated. He specifically mentioned that white students were withdrawn and, for example, not running for student council. (The school was located in a white neighborhood, but its student body was more than 60 percent minority; to protect students from sometimes hostile residents, all were bused to school.)

The planning team worked with RBS on program development until RBS assistance was withdrawn during the second year because of funding cuts. The group made relatively little progress; they developed goals and described ways to attain some. The only identifiable project outcomes were several changes introduced or reinstituted by the principal—for example, the student council was reorganized to include equal representation from each ethnic group, the discipline code was revised, and academic and behavioral award systems were introduced.

Serious problems were encountered at Urban almost from the beginning. First, teachers were very skeptical, bordering on hostile. They doubted that RBS could help them. This was at least partially due to previous unproductive work with external consultants. Teachers objected to the process used to develop the innovation; they wondered whether RBS employees understood inner-city schools. During the fourth project meeting, a key participant who was chairperson of a major department criticized the process by saying, "You are treating me like a six year old. . . . In view of all our problems, I'll be retired and we'll still be shuffling cards." Other planning team members picked up on the criticisms. One asked questions about "the objective of this managerial model you have us going through." Later, a third teacher said, "Most of us don't want our values clarified; nor do we want theory. . . . We know our values and what we want. . . . The message we are trying to deliver is that we should get to the nitty-gritty."

Second, while the program addressed some of the principal's priorities, other planning team members felt that other problems were more important. One person named physical factors she considered to be explanations for student discipline problems (lack of sleep, poor diets, and a poorly heated school building) and said that if RBS could not solve those problems she was wasting her time at meetings. Third, the school lacked resources to relieve planning team members of teaching duties during project meetings; therefore, sessions were limited to 45-minute class periods; even then, some teachers were usually unable to attend. Fourth, factions existed within the school. Arguments between planning team members sometimes disrupted meetings.

Largely because of these contextual factors, RBS field agents eventually became skeptical that innovation development and implementation would be successful in Urban; waiting for the fourth meeting to begin, one field agent said to another that he wished the principal would tell them if he "wants RBS to go away." Thus, the collaborative efforts at Urban seemed doomed almost from the start.

BIGTOWN HIGH SCHOOL

Bigtown adopted the career education project shortly after hiring a district career education coordinator. That person became RBS' main contact at the site and assumed major responsibility for the project. When the planning began, a large team was selected. Its approximately 15 members included the career education coordinator, the principal, a district administrator, four department chairpersons, a counselor, a board member who later became president, a community representative who later became mayor, and two students.

The group's size and composition made productive work difficult. Members were interested in career education and department chairpersons wanted a voice in changes that would affect them, but most members did not care to be involved in the more mundane work of actually developing a program.

Consequently, a smaller working group that included only half of the planning team was formed to work with the career education coordinator and RBS field agent. They developed plans that were then submitted to the entire committee.

The second year, a new RBS field agent again tried to work with the larger committee, but without success. By this time interest had waned, and it was even difficult to convene meetings. As each meeting began, a secretary frantically called members to remind them to attend. Not knowing about the second working group, the field agent met with the career education coordinator to develop such program components as goals, objectives, and performance statements. When they reached the stage of writing classroom activities, a group of classroom teachers was contracted for that task. The state department of education provided money to pay the teachers. They wrote activities, pilot tested them, and revised them during the summer.

The nature of RBS' work with Bigtown changed during the third year, primarily because of a state department initiative that mandated graduation requirements in career education. Districts were to identify "proficiencies" and describe how they would be met. As at Oldtown, Bigtown administrators decided to use the work with RBS to satisfy those requirements. Subsequently, the career education coordinator and RBS field agent worked with committees of teachers to write proficiencies and activities that would be inserted into district curricula.

Incentives played a particularly major role in project events at Bigtown. Before the project even began, the district had sufficient incentives, through state legislation supporting career education, to hire a jobs placement counselor whose responsibilities included career education. That person was expected to produce a career education curriculum and was motivated to spend many hours working on it with RBS. The planning team did not have sufficient incentives to actually do the development work, although department chairpersons wanted veto power. The group that wrote activities was lured by money; in exchange, they had a contractual commitment to write and pilot test the activities. Then, the state mandate for career education gave the district an incentive to use and extend the work that had already been completed, as well as to continue to take advantage of the RBS field agent's assistance. Finally, the inclusion of career education in district curricula was expected to give teachers sufficient incentives to implement the activities.

NEIGHBORTOWN HIGH SCHOOL

District administrators in this rural community eagerly accepted RBS' invitation to participate in the career education project. They were interested in giving their high school students (most of whom had had limited exposure to a wide array of occupations) an introduction to the many options available. Plus, they could not resist receiving the technical assistance RBS offered at no cost. "The best help we've ever had," one official concluded. "It's a shame it wasn't in science or math." And therein lies the key to an apparent paradox. Neighbortown participants in the project were generally cooperative, active, and supportive; and yet, the field agents' and participants' intentions never reached fruition. There simply came a time when district officials could not justify allocating so much staff time to the district's third or fourth priority. Teachers interpreted this as a lack of administrator interest and as a signal that their effort was not highly valued.

None of this would have been predicted by participants early on. The original committee members—two appointed teachers, the principal, the director of guidance, the mayor, a student, and a district administrator—quickly reached a consensus that career education was important. Although the mayor's and student's attendance was spotty, the remaining members enthusiastically participated in each meeting during the first year. They surveyed faculty and the community about appropriate goals and reached agreement on what the most important of these were. The field agent led the meetings—an arrangement with which everyone was openly comfortable.

The second year was devoted to designing classroom activities and testing them. The committee was expanded to include four additional teachers so that each of the five major departments had at least one representative (English, math, science, social studies, and business). Because the project focus had shifted from school goals to classroom activities, the nonteacher members were not present at these work sessions. Instead, they moved into more of an advisory capacity.

The RBS field agent was doubly busy. There were the meetings to plan, coordinate, and lead. Moreover, the committee decided to implement two new career education courses, and the teachers selected to handle these had limited career education experience. The field agent, as a result, had to train these people and assist the design of the courses.

At this point, the project was essentially completed. Teachers had their classroom activities designed; the courses were in place and attracting students. The field agent continued to be "on call" for the teachers running the special courses, but for all practical purposes the school was on its own during the third year. Research visits to Neighbortown later in the year found little of the earlier excitement and uncovered some confusion about what had happened. Teachers reported they felt the administrators had dropped the project; administrators reported they felt the project was successful and the ball was now in the teachers' court.

Events at Neighbortown provided some important insights into the change process. They illustrated the critical nature of administrator encouragement after the formal project ended. Its absence defused what, by all indications, was destined to be a successful project. A corollary was that the district found it difficult to continue to push any priorities beyond the first or second ones. Thus, there was a relationship between the project's priority in the district and whether administrator encouragement was forthcoming. An additional insight this site yielded was variance in the nature of subunits' organization within a school. In fact, the observation of this at Neighbortown spurred a more systematic examination in the other sites.

OLDTOWN HIGH SCHOOL

The RBS project coordinator, an assistant principal, was a busy person. She handled the testing program for the high school's 3,000 plus students, coordinated curriculum development activities, and arranged workshops—all of this in addition to the myriad everyday activities the Oldtown administrators faced. Indeed, sitting in her cluttered office on the first floor of the aged school building, one typically would find a conversation interrupted in rapid sequence by parent calls, student visits, and teacher queries. Those who worked with this administrator uniformly expressed praise for her thoroughness and professionalism despite the hectic schedule.

The RBS field agent felt fortunate to work with such a person. From the start, the coordinator took full responsibility for running the planning meetings. The coordinator was convinced that for the career education project to be successful, school staff members had to do it themselves. The two teachers, three district administrators, and community representative on the committee came to accept this view as well. The field agent, as a result, was able to perform much as intended—as an advisor and resource finder rather than a full-time leader.

At the end of the first year, after the committee had reached agreement on project goals, the state education agency announced a grants competition for career education programs. Fighting a tight deadline, the field agent and project coordinator huddled to write a proposal for the one-year funding. The effort was successful, and the whole committee felt it was a compliment to their work that the money was awarded. However, certain stipulations about the need for staff development in the grants announcement meant that the project would follow a slightly different path. Instead of continuing the committee's systematic planning, effort would be shifted to organizing a series of workshops to help teachers plan classroom-level career education activities.

The project, initially, did not adhere to the schedule contained in the proposal. The coordinator had to organize and implement a new lesson plan program for all teachers and was unable to devote any time to career education. By late fall, however, the reporting procedures spelled out in the proposal demanded that the RBS effort receive attention. Three teachers met with the coordinator to plan the workshops and 20 teacher volunteers were selected to participate. The field agent remained involved as a content expert.

By the beginning of the third year, the activities required in the proposal had been completed. Because of other responsibilities, the coordinator once again had to relinquish the time that had been devoted to career education. The RBS project ended at this point. The coordinator expressed regrets about this because she felt strongly that teachers deserved continued praise for their innovative efforts. Serendipidously, the state subsequently mandated high school graduation requirements in career education. This reshuffled the coordinator's priorities enough that she felt that she could devote more time to recommending project-related changes as ways for teachers to comply with the state's policy.

Overall, the project had moderate success at Oldtown, according to the coordinator. Oldtown was an interesting case because events there suggested that building local ownership of a project and having an administrator as an ardent supporter did not ensure widespread success. The committee and the coordinator had to work in a larger context that placed constraints on the time they had available. Thus, individual actors were not always free to carry out their intentions in the ways they wanted. There also was an organizational barrier at Oldtown to spreading change beyond the workshop participants. As discussed in Chapter 6, teachers had few opportunities to talk to other members of their departments because of a split schedule. This meant that only briefly during the day were all teachers physically present at the same time.

APPENDIX B
Description
of Research Methods

The research for this study spanned three school years. During that time the focus and intensity of fieldwork varied considerably. A team of researchers began working in individual sites when the first meetings between RBS staff and school district personnel were held. Researchers attended most project meetings that year but tended not to visit the schools at other times. During the second year, the research team decided that to obtain a better understanding of project events more in-depth investigation was needed. Thus, field visits became more frequent and were concerned with general school operation as well as the projects themselves. Because of limited resources, however, only five sites could be studied in depth. A researcher was responsible for one or two sites and visited each approximately once or twice a week. In the third year of the study, researchers continued to cover project activities at the five sites but concentrated most of the research effort on interviewing staff in all 14 sites. For all three years, the research team maintained steady interaction with RBS field agents.

The composition of the research team varied over time. During the first year, four researchers conducted most of the site visits. Only one had been trained in field work methods; the others had been drawn from other RBS units. Before the beginning of the second year, the person who had field work training was appointed director of the research unit and hired three trained field researchers—with backgrounds in sociology of education, anthropology, and educational research and evaluation. They conducted all the field work during the second year. At the beginning of the third year, one fieldworker left to finish a dissertation; the other two did the remaining field work.

DATA COLLECTION

The major intent of the research was to study the influence of local school contextual conditions on the process and outcomes of the change projects. Initially, the research was exploratory. That is, it was to generate hypotheses about the process (Glaser and Strauss, 1967). Research later moved beyond this objective and was able to discipline the ideas. This type of research, it was felt, could be accomplished best through an open-ended research approach that would not restrict data collection to information specified in advance. Consequently, qualitative research procedures were used. The major data collection methods were observation and interviewing. Other sources of data included a questionnaire, demographic data, field agent contact reports, and documents. They will all be described below.

Observation

Researchers attended meetings of project planning teams as well as smaller meetings between RBS field agents and others, such as school and district administrators and local project coordinators. Researchers also observed school faculty meetings, informal interaction in public areas of schools (e.g., faculty lounges, dining rooms, hallways, and principals' offices), school board meetings, and teachers' classrooms.

The observations were unstructured; researchers did not limit their observations or field notes to particular behaviors or events. Instead, they attempted to record meetings or other interactions as thoroughly and with as little inference as possible. Initially, researchers focused on verbal interaction during meetings and attempted to record all remarks verbatim. Obviously that goal was not attainable, but the emphasis remained on capturing conversations and events as closely as possible. As the study progressed, observations became more highly focused. Researchers' knowledge of the settings, the data that had already been collected, and issues they intended to pursue allowed them to select out that information that was most important to record. Observation became less frequent in the final year of the study as the team shifted to conducting interviews with staff at all 14 sites.

Researchers were nonparticipant observers. They sat with participants at meeting tables and made notes but did not take part in formal discussions. Although participants knew the researchers and why they were there, they generally did not interact with them during meetings. The relationships among researchers, field agents, and participants were comfortable; they interacted with one another before and after meetings, during other visits to schools, and at RBS. During meetings, field agents and participants sometimes jokingly said to researchers such things as "Did you get that?" (i.e., had they recorded a particular remark) or if a compliment was afforded someone, invariably the target of the exchange turned to the researcher and said, "Make sure you write that down."

Interviewing

Interviewing was the second major source of research information. Over the course of the study, the researchers conducted a great variety of interviews. The people interviewed included program participants, nonparticipating staff members, school- and district-level administrators, a few students, and field agents. Some interviews were scheduled in advance; researchers made appointments to meet people at a designated time and place. Other interviews occurred spontaneously as opportunities arose to talk with people in areas of the school where they tended to congregate, before or after project meetings, at RBS, or in transit to and from meetings. Spontaneous interviews were generally conversational in tone and researchers used lines of questioning that seemed nonthreatening in the situation or permitted probing into matters discussed previously. Sometimes researchers collected information by eavesdropping; for example, they listened to and later recorded events that occurred as they waited near principals' offices or sat in faculty lounges.

The extent to which the interviews were structured in advance varied. None were "highly structured"—that is, neither the way in which questions were worded nor the way responses were categorized were specified in advance. However, researchers knew the general kinds of information they intended to collect. During interviews conducted early in the study, researchers obtained background information about each participant; for example, they asked questions about career history, previous experience in similar projects, and motivations for participating. In the second year, interviews were loosely structured as researchers attempted to learn about such issues as the demands placed on participants by the projects, people's reactions to the innovations, school policies and procedures, and interrelationships among school personnel. Staff were interviewed as both subjects and informants. As the study progressed, however, interviews became more focused. Researchers asked questions to pursue particular lines of inquiry generated by interim analyses—for example, the influence of various structuring mechanisms on participation or implementation, the incentives and disincentives that affected participants, the influence of various administrative behaviors on projects, and the nature of changes that had been made. The research team compared what data were available from different sites and generated research questions to be answered either through existing field notes or in subsequent interviews. This was particularly important near the end of the study to insure that comparable data would be available across all sites.

Survey

A survey was administered in the first year of the study to all teachers (participants and nonparticipants) in 13 sites. It was administered one year later in Middletown because the school did not enter the study until that time. The survey asked teachers about such things as their perceptions of the relative importance of specific goals; the degree of influence they had over particular decision areas relative to the principal, central office, and school board; and the existence and enforcement of several types of policies. More detailed information on this survey is contained in Firestone and Herriott (1981a).

Demographic Data

Demographic data were collected from all schools. The data included number of students and staff members, racial composition, reading achievement levels, and rate of enrollment . decline.

Field Agent Contact Reports

Some field agents routinely filed "contact reports" with their respective RBS components after each site visit. Researchers requested copies of some of those reports, especially when they could not be present during a site visit. The contact reports contained such information as objectives of the visit, descriptions of the flow of events, identification of critical issues to be resolved, and the outcomes of the visit.

Documents

Researchers collected a variety of documents during the study. Documents from schools included newspaper articles, curriculum outlines, within-school notices, and program descriptions. RBS documents were primarily project proposals, materials prepared for use in schools, and descriptions of the approaches for developing programs.

Techniques for Insuring Validity

Researchers used several techniques during the data collection stage to help insure that data were valid (Dawson, 1982).

Basically, they attempted (1) to establish research conditions that were favorable for validity, (2) to continually question the accuracy of data, and (3) to subject their perceptions and interpretations to the scrutiny of others.

Two major research conditions helped improve validity: spending extensive time in sites and establishing favorable relationships with informants. The researchers' extensive presence in five of the schools contributed to validity in several ways. The researchers were able to collect more data to inform their opinions (Greene and David, 1981), to test their interpretations many times in many ways (Becker, 1970), to become sufficiently acquainted with people to interpret their comments accurately (Bruyn, 1966), and to avoid collecting too much data at unrepresentative times (Bogdan and Taylor, 1975). In comparison to 25 other multisite qualitative studies surveyed by Firestone and Herriott (1982), this study ranked among those rated "high" in on-site presence.

Researchers continually monitored their relationships with informants, though most relationships were positive from the beginning. Researchers convinced field agents that they were studying the process of change and were not evaluating the agents' work (although this did not always turn out to be the case as published documents were occasionally used by the components to assess their work). Nevertheless, the field agents became comfortable in the researchers' presence, welcomed them to attend even small planning meetings, and confided in them. In some sites, researchers knew that informants' remarks should not get back to certain people (usually administrators) and assured them of confidentiality. Informants learned they could trust the researchers and rarely, to researchers' knowledge, withheld information they thought could be used against them.

Researchers continually questioned the accuracy of data and the credibility of informants. One program participant, for example, seemed to relish giving a researcher the "inside scoop" on matters such as interrelationships among staff members or events surrounding an administrator who was in trouble with central office staff. Although most of that information was later confirmed, none was used until it had been verified.

Researchers frequently filed away—often in their heads—information that required independent confirmation.

Intersubjective confirmation of data occurred during the data collection stage when researchers discussed their observations and interpretations with others who knew the settings, primarily research colleagues and field agents. They offered rival interpretations of the data, sometimes based on their experiences with other sites.

DATA MANAGEMENT

Field notes were recorded after each site visit and each conversation with a field agent at RBS. Researchers dictated the notes into a tape recorder; secretaries transcribed the notes. A common format was used for all notes so that certain information would consequently be located in the same places in a report. For example, researchers specified at the beginning of the field notes the names of participants and purposes of meetings and usually saved interpretations of events until the end. Interpretations in the body of the report were enclosed in parentheses.

A computerized coding system was used to index the field notes so that they would be readily accessible. Codes indicated whether data referred to RBS, the school, its environment, the change process, or program outcomes. Within each, numerous codes existed to help identify the data more specifically. The codes were then entered into a computer record, so that they could be easily indexed and accessed. The data were later collated on printouts according to code so that researchers could easily locate all field note references to a particular topic.

Several measures were taken during the data management stage to ensure validity. Field notes were recorded as soon as possible after each site visit. The notes included as much detail as possible. As mentioned previously, researchers attempted to minimize inference. They distinguished between observations and interpretations. Researchers read their field notes after transcription and before coding. In all, over 3,500 pages of field notes were generated during the three years.

DATA ANALYSIS

At an informal level, data analysis was continuous. It began as researchers collected data, recorded field notes, and read them. In doing so, researchers saw patterns and recurring themes. For example, the effects of school resources on participation became apparent as teachers from several schools repeatedly came to project meetings frustrated about leaving their students with substitutes they knew would not provide good instruction or missed meetings because substitutes were not available. The use of ordinary knowledge to make decisions became evident as participants talked about having made classroom changes before data from sequential-planning procedures were available.

At a formal level, researchers analyzed data at the end of each year and prepared interim reports of study findings. At the end of the first year, field data were used to answer sets of questions devised by the research team about project events and the schools. Schools were then rated on several variables— for example, frequency of field agent contact, participant ownership of project, and progress through the planning process. Discussions about these ratings enabled researchers to see more systematic patterns in the data than informal analysis allowed.

At the end of the second year, researchers identified several topics for analysis that seemed to help explain project events. The topics included field agent roles, administrative support for innovation, and organizational linkages. Individual researchers analyzed the data on one or two topics and wrote interim reports.

During the first stage of analysis for this report, researchers reviewed the field notes from the sites and wrote brief site summaries that described and explained program outcomes. Concurrently, the researchers decided to pursue a major finding that had emerged over time—that local school conditions substantially influenced planning, implementation, and continuation.

The analysis techniques used in this report varied somewhat by chapter. However, analysis always resembled the comparative case study method (Yin, 1981). Researchers started either with an aspect of the change process or an outcome and worked backward to the influence of school context. Patterns of events were first examined by site. Then, efforts were made to locate commonalities across the sites.

For example, in Chapter 4, on sequential planning, prior knowledge of departures from the process served as a starting point for analysis. In one school, teachers identified problems in their classrooms that reduced time-on-task and made adjustments before that stage of the planning process had been reached; teachers in another school made changes to improve discipline rather than to reduce transition time between activities, even though data indicated the former was less of a problem. Criteria that would indicate that the process had been followed in other sites were then established. Knowledge of the sites, the field notes, and research team discussions identified departures from the process and reasons for their occurrence. These reasons were then categorized. Local conditions were major explanatory factors. Some conditions coincided with initial explanations in analyses of other issues; others were redefined in light of that analysis.

In Chapter 6, on implementation, analysis started with an assessment of the quantity of implementation. To get an estimate of this, field notes were used to identify the number of teachers who made classroom changes. On the basis of analyses in previous reports, the decision was made to focus on the influence of one condition that seemed the most critical to how widely a school changed: the existence of linkages within schools or departments. Then knowledge of the sites as well as additional information from field notes were used to explain how linkages influenced the spread of change.

During the analyses, researchers prepared various kinds of tables and charts, many of which are included in this book. "Data display charts" (Huberman and Miles, 1982) described each site with respect to particular variables. Other charts contained numbers or ratings. The tables and charts were used primarily to present data in a way that would permit researchers and readers to quickly grasp site-specific or cross-site information, to identify relationships among variables, and to gauge the extent to which particular findings were true for all sites.

REPORTING

As indicated in the previous section, reports were written at the end of each year of the study. All reports went through a multiple-stage reviewing process and were revised after each stage; the major purposes of the reviews were to reexamine interpretations and control the quality of reports. Reviewers during the first stage included other members of the research team and other researchers in their organizational unit of RBS. Second-stage reviewers included other members of RBS, primarily developers, field agents, and administrators. Third-stage reviewers were external to RBS and included members of the study advisory committee.

APPENDIX C
Analyzing a School

The premise of this report is that field agents can more effectively provide assistance to schools if they understand the nature and potential influence of local contextual conditions and adjust their strategies or manipulate the conditions accordingly. The intent of this appendix is to suggest to field agents what to look for in schools to assess the potential influence of school conditions and how to look for it.

WHAT TO LOOK FOR

Field agents need to have up-to-date knowledge of the status of contextual conditions in a particular school. That means they should deliberately seek such knowledge before beginning a project and continually monitor the situation to insure that the knowledge is current. The remainder of this section suggests the kinds of information field agents can use to identify and understand the conditions discussed in this report. The conditions, obviously, are not exhaustive of all of those that can affect the change process. Field agents should remain alert to other intervening factors as well.

181

Availability of Resources

The availability of school resources is likely to influence the amount of time that staff members are able and willing to devote to a program. Teachers' schedules often leave little time for them to meet as groups to make plans for educational change. Resources may also be needed to hire substitutes or to pay teachers to attend meetings after school. Field agents may want to examine the feasibility of other alternatives—enlisting personnel with more flexible schedules (counselors or specialists, for example) as participants or having nonparticipants cover classes during meetings. Gathering the following types of information should help field agents as they attempt to minimize the influence of resource availability on innovation planning and implementation.

Teachers.   To what extent are teachers available to participate in planning? Do they have planning periods or other time that can be used flexibly? Do enough teachers have planning periods in common to arrange meetings then? Are teachers available after school to attend meetings? Do administrators feel comfortable asking teachers to relinquish planning or other "free" time to attend meetings? When do "busy seasons" (reporting and testing periods, major holidays, end-of-year activities) occur?

Other Staff.   What employees (e.g., assistant administrators, specialists, counselors) have flexible schedules that allow them to participate with a minimum of disruption to the school? Who is available to handle such details as scheduling meetings, reserving meeting rooms, notifying participants, and providing clerical/typing assistance? Who has or is willing to obtain expertise in the area of the innovation? Are they also willing/able to assist other participants? Are others available to cover participants' classrooms during project meetings?

Administrators.   To what extent are administrators willing and able to participate actively, attend meetings, and talk with participants about the project at other times? Does the principal have an assistant to relieve him or her of duties that might otherwise impinge upon the principal's involvement in the project? Is an administrator available to assume project leadership—*if* that is wise in a given situation? To what extent is the administrator willing to devote school resources to the project, or does he or she consider other things more important?

Substitute Teachers. Is money available to pay substitutes? If not, can it be obtained from other sources? What is the school or district's practice regarding using substitutes to free teachers to do development work? Are substitutes available in sufficient quantity? Do teachers consider them competent? If long meetings are to be held frequently or over a long period of time, can substitutes be contracted and assigned to the same classrooms throughout the project?

Money. Is money also available for other purposes? To purchase materials and equipment? To pay teachers for working on nonschool time or during the summer? To purchase refreshments for project meetings? To duplicate project materials? To hire consultants?

Incentives and Disincentives for Involvement

People's perceptions of incentives or disincentives for participating in program planning and implementation may influence their willingness to do so. If, for example, participants expect to be evaluated more favorably as a result of participating in a project or relish the opportunity to discuss professional matters with peers, they are likely to be more willing to devote scarce time to a program. On the other hand, if disincentives are high (e.g., if participation threatens the quality of instruction students receive), people may be less willing to be involved. Questions that field agents might ask about incentives and disincentives follow.

Role in Teacher Evaluation. Is mere participation likely to lead to a more favorable evaluation or to avoidance of a negative one? For example, are all teachers expected to participate in extra projects? Might implementation influence a teacher's evaluation? Is the innovation such that administrators could use it to evaluate teachers? If so, are they likely to do so?

Other Perceived Rewards. Will people receive in-service credit or money for participating? Might the project help advance their careers (e.g., through publicity, increased contact with administrators, opportunities to exhibit leadership)? Are resulting changes likely to increase student achievement or motivation? Are some participants especially concerned about or interested in the content of the innovation? Do people value the opportunity for increased professional contact with colleagues, administrators, or outside experts?

Contribution to Meeting External Requirements. What state or district mandates or expectations can the innovation help participants meet? What school person(s) are most responsible for ensuring that the requirements are met (principal, curriculum coordinator, language arts specialist)? What additional requirements are anticipated in the future?

Detraction from Other Responsibilities. How does spending time in meetings or implementing an innovation reduce the extent to which participants can meet their other responsibilities? Do they feel they are depriving students by leaving them with a person who is less likely to provide a valuable learning experience? Are people concerned that they will be less likely to cover a particular body of content? Do administrators or teachers fear that the time is not well spent?

Imposition on Nonparticipants. In what ways does the project impose on nonparticipants? Are they asked to relinquish their time to cover participants' classes or to accept additional students? Are special classes cancelled, leaving more students in classrooms or depriving nonparticipants of free periods? How extensive are those impositions? How have nonparticipants reacted to them? How have those reactions influenced participants?

Nature of School Structure

The extent to which work-related activities are interdependent varies widely within as well as between schools. For example, teaching activities may be much more closely coordinated in one department than another; or the content that is taught may be highly specified but not the activities used to teach it. In some schools, a principal's mandate to change may insure immediate implementation; in others the principal may not be sanguine about teachers' responses to such an issuance. Therefore, field agents and others who want to identify potential influences on change projects, especially how widely changes get implemented, need to be alert to differences within and between schools.

Coordination of Teaching. Do teachers plan lessons together, or at least keep one another closely informed about what they are teaching? To what extent does that occur in various grade levels, departments, or other organizational units? Is the school—or portions of it—organized into teams? What teachers plan together informally? When teachers coordinate with one another, what do they coordinate? Content? Methods? Lessons for particular days? Tests? If one teacher wants to make a change, how does he or she arrange it with others?

Formal Curricula. What formal curricula exist in the school? What subject areas do they cover? To what extent are teachers expected to follow the curricula? Do they comply with those expectations? How detailed are the curricula? Do they name the specific materials or methods that are to be used? Are teachers able to use content/materials/methods that are not in the curricula? Do they have time to do so? What are the procedures for changing the curricula?

Interaction with Administrators. How extensively do teachers talk with school administrators about school concerns? What do they talk about? Under what circumstances—for example, during informal interaction before or after school, common planning periods, and faculty meetings or only at times of evaluations? How often do evaluations occur? How are they perceived by teachers?

Agreement About Goals and Priorities. What evidence exists that certain goals are particularly important at the present time? Does the school have a "mission" that staff members are aware of and to which they agree? What themes echo through in-service sessions, posters, or slogans? What other special projects has the school adopted?

School Priorities

The amount of compatibility between school and project goals and priorities may influence teachers' and administrators' willingness to devote time and other resources to a project. People are more inclined to work on a project that contributes to the achievement of important school goals than one that either does not or detracts from them. Questions in the above section on agreement about goals and priorities can help a field agent identify those which are most important; other questions that will provide information about school goals and priorities follow.

Identification. What are the major school goals? What is the relative priority of each? What are the perceived major problems of the school? How does the innovation address them?

The Match with a Project. How and why did the school become involved in the project? How does the project address school priorities and problems? If the project addresses goals/problems that are of low priority, has an administrator strongly endorsed it? Has he/she informed staff members that working on it is important—even if it means temporarily neglecting other goals?

Factions

School factions can disrupt the planning process and make it difficult for people to work together cooperatively. Meetings may sometimes have to be devoted to dealing with those problems. A project can become identified with one particular group, creating resistance to the changes among opposing groups. Questions that may help field agents understand the factions present in a particular school are included below.

Their Nature. What factions or tensions exist within a school? Is the faculty split into dissenting groups? Do tensions exist between faculty and school administrators? The district offices? The school board? What is the relationship between the teachers' association or union and others? What is the status of the teachers' contract? Are there tensions that involve the community? Students? How did the groups develop? Do they revolve around particular issues?

Factions and Projects. Who is aligned with what sides? Who belongs to what factions or cliques? Where do various groups stand in relation to one another? How strong are the tensions? Are they so strong that people even have difficulty participating in meetings together or working together in situations that might be construed as evaluative?

Staff Turnover

The rate of staff turnover in a school can be indicative of a number of possible conditions in the school. For example, it can point to uncertainty over what direction a school or district should take, concern over poor working conditions, or even such good working conditions that the district is a stepping stone for more prestigious positions. Regardless, staff turnover can seriously affect a project. For example, a key project advocate may leave the school and create a need for additional advocates. A participant with important responsibilities may leave and create a void. Field agents can learn about staff turnover by looking into the following questions.

The Rate. What proportion of the staff has been at the school for at least three years? Five? Ten? What proportion has spent most of their careers in the building? How long has the principal been there? The superintendent? Where in the school (grade levels, departments) are the relatively new staff members?

Potential Effects on a Project. At the beginning of a new school year, what participants are no longer at the school? What needs do their absences create? Do their project roles need to be filled by someone else? How important is it to obtain the support of their successors? Who are the new staff members? What expectations do they/others have regarding their participation in the project?

Current Practices

Implementing innovations will require that some participants depart further from their everyday patterns of behavior than others. Some people are so accustomed to behaving in a particular manner that changing it would almost require ignoring their instincts and following procedures in which they have less confidence. Some of the questions a field agent may want to answer in order to learn about a school's current practices are as follows.

Departures from Customary Practice. What current practices of participants are likely to be influenced by the project and related changes—for example, teaching methods, decision-making processes, styles of working together? How different are those current practices from what they should be after the change is implemented? How does the magnitude of the differences vary among participants? What difficulties may participants encounter in changing their practices?

The Extent to Which Customary Practices Are Ingrained. Is the project designed to influence behaviors that are very natural to participants, that are an integral part of their everyday actions? That is, does the project affect core practices or peripheral practices, from the participants' perspectives?

Prior Projects

The prior history of innovative projects in a school may influence staff members' attitudes toward new projects or field agents. For example, they may be hesitant to commit time and energy to a project because they suspect that, within a year or two, administrators will discontinue supporting it in favor of something else that comes along. Or, they may be skeptical that outsiders will be able to help them. Questions that field agents might want to ask about prior projects include the following.

Their Nature.   What other projects were attempted during the last 3–5 years? What happened to them? Why?

Their Legacy.   Do staff members have a particular attitude toward new projects? For example, do they think the principal adopts many programs—to receive favorable attention from the superintendent or community—but does not follow through on them? Do they think that outsiders are unlikely to understand their situation or to offer suggestions they have not already considered?

BECOMING INFORMED ABOUT SCHOOL CONDITIONS

Obtaining answers to all the questions suggested in the previous section would, of course, be very time consuming. Field agents need to decide what types of information are most important to collect in a particular situation. They will then need to allocate time to acquiring the information as part of the preparation process that occurs before beginning work in a new site. They will also probably want to collect some data deliberately during the early stages of a project and to remain alert to other information later. Of course, multiple strategies will be necessary to obtain the information, such as interviewing participants and administrators, listening to people (participants and nonparticipants) and talking to them informally in school corridors and teachers' lounges, relying on informants, and examining various documents.

Interviews can be scheduled with administrators and participants before a project; also, field agents can ask about the school during preliminary meetings or working sessions. While some field agents may feel uncomfortable asking a lot of questions because they feel it is a task more appropriate for researchers, school administrators and participants may see the questions as evidence that the field agent is interested in them. Some people seem to be gratified that an outsider who works with many people in many schools is genuinely interested in them. However, field agents will need to avoid asking questions that are threatening and that suggest they are judging people's performances as teachers or administrators. These data collection activities are particularly useful for learning about such things as school resources, participants' schedules, school problems or goals that are currently especially important, and staff turnover.

Spending time in hallways, project meeting rooms, cafeterias, principals' outer offices, and playgrounds is sometimes a very useful way to learn about a school. A field agent can talk to people informally or eavesdrop on other conversations. Of course, it is necessary to be careful about relaying that information to other people, whether they are internal or external to a school. Also, field agents who spend too much unstructured time in a setting can appear to have little else to do; arriving slightly early for an appointment or a meeting is a way to add legitimacy to this activity.

Cultivating informants who will provide sensitive information that may be difficult to obtain from others—for example, the existence of interpersonal tensions or controversies that people are hesitant to talk about—can also be useful. Sometimes field agents can acquire data from informants that would take months to get through other means. When using informants, at least two precautions must be taken. First, the field agent must be careful to avoid having other people identify him or her with the informant. Field agents usually do not want to align themselves with any particular individuals or group. Second, field agents should not accept information from in-

formants as true before confirming it independently. People
who are eager to provide information may be driven to fabri-
cate it occasionally. Thus, information must be triangulated.
For example, during this study a potential informant volun-
teered information of a "gossipy" nature. During an initial
interview, the informant identified a particular clique within
the school. Before accepting the information as accurate, the
researcher observed the supposed members of the clique during nonclass time (e.g., during lunch or after school) and
listened to what others said about them. These sources of
information confirmed the initial comment. With this knowledge, the researcher could avoid becoming overly identified
with any one faction. To preserve this neutrality, the informant
was approached only during interviews that were scheduled as
part of a cycle of interviews with all participants or briefly while
scheduling the interviews.

Several kinds of documents may contain useful information
about school context. Such documents include printed curricula, written rules or procedures, school or district newsletters,
and local newspaper articles about the school.

Whatever methods of collecting information are used, field
agents should gather information before a project begins and
then continually expand and update it. To repeat once again, a
field agent who is aware of the contextual conditions in a
particular school can reduce their effects by adjusting his or
her actions or attempting to alter the conditions. Certainly,
field agents always seek to know their clients better; what this
appendix has done is to reiterate what information is likely to
be most important to have and to suggest some ways to gather it
more systematically.

About the Authors

H. Dickson Corbett is a Senior Research Associate in the Field Studies Component of Research for Better Schools, Philadelphia, Pennsylvania. His research areas of specialization are organizational theory, planned educational change, qualitative research methods, and teacher training. He has published numerous articles in professional journals and presented papers at professional meetings. His teaching experience included both junior high and college. He received his Ph.D. degree from the University of North Carolina, Chapel Hill.

Judith A. Dawson serves as Research Associate at Research for Better Schools. Her major research interests are educational program evaluation, qualitative and quantitative research methods, and planned educational change. She has presented her findings at professional meetings and published in professional journals. For four years she taught kindergarten in Illinois. Her Ph.D. degree is from the University of Illinois.

William A. Firestone is Director of Field Studies, Research for Better Schools, where he has been responsible for studies of educational change processes, school organizational and administrative processes, and ways in which external agencies contribute to school improvement. He has also taught at the college level. The recipient of a Ford Urban Studies Fellowship, he received his Ph.D. degree from the University of

Chicago. His publications include *Great Expectations for Small Schools: The Limitations of Federal Projects* and numerous journal articles and research reports.

References

Allison, G. T. *Essence of decision.* Boston: Little, Brown, 1971.

Baldridge, J. V., & Burnham, R. A. Organizational innovation: individual, organizational, and environmental impacts. *Administrative Science Quarterly,* 1975, *20,* 165–176.

Baldridge, J. V., & Deal, T. E. *Managing change in educational organizations.* Berkeley, CA: McCutchan, 1975.

Bartunek, J. M., & Keys, C. B. Participation in school decision making. *Urban Education,* 1979, *14*(1), 52–75.

Becker, H. S. *Sociological work: Method and substance.* Chicago: Aldine, 1970.

Benjamin, R. *Making schools work.* New York: Continuum, 1981.

Berman, P. Toward an implementation paradigm. In R. Lehming and M. Kane (Eds.), *Improving schools: Using what we know.* Beverly Hills, CA: Sage, 1981.

Berman, P., & McLaughlin, M. Implementation of educational innovation. *Educational Forum,* 1976, *40*(3), 345–370.

Berman, P., & McLaughlin, M. *Federal programs supporting educational change: Vol. 7. Factors affecting implementation and continuation.* Santa Monica, CA: Rand, 1977.

Blumberg, A. Teachers, other teachers and principals: Welds and cracks in the couplings. Paper presented at the annual meeting of the American Educational Research Association, Boston, 1980.

Bogdan, R., & Taylor, S. J. *Introduction to qualitative research methods: A phenomenological approach to the social sciences.* New York: Wiley, 1975.

Brickell, H. M. How to change what matters. *Educational Leadership,* 1980, *34*(3), 202–207.

195

Bruyn, S. T. The human perspective in sociology: The methodology of participant observation. Englewood Cliffs, NJ: Prentice-Hall, 1966.

Campbell, D. T. Qualitative knowing in action research. Paper presented at the annual meeting of the American Psychological Association, New Orleans, 1974.

Chabotar, K. J., Louis, K. S., & Sjogren, J. *Relationships between local contributions and the success of a federal school improvement program.* Cambridge, MA: Abt Associates, 1981.

Charters, W. W., & Pellegrin, R. Barriers to the innovation process: Four case studies of differentiated staffing. *Administrative Science Quarterly*, 1973, *9*, 3–14.

Clark, D. L. In consideration of goal-free planning: The failure of traditional planning systems in education. *Educational Administration Quarterly*, 1981, *17*(3), 42–60.

Coch, L., & French, J. Overcoming resistance to change. *Human Relations*, 1948, *11*, 512–532.

Corbett, H. D. To make an omelette you have to break the egg crate. *Educational Leadership*, 1982, *40*(2), 34–35. (a)

Corbett, H. D. Principals' contributions to maintaining change. *Phi Delta Kappan*, 1982, *64*(3), 190–192. (b)

Corwin, R. G. Innovation in organizations: The case of schools. *Sociology of Education*, 1975, *48*, 1–37.

Corwin, R. G. Patterns of organizational control and teacher militancy: Theoretical continuities in the idea of "loose coupling." In R. G. Corwin (Ed.), *Research in sociology of education and socialization: Vol. 2. Research on educational organizations.* Greenwich, CT: JAI Press, 1981.

Crandall, D. P., Bouchner, J. E., Loucks, S. F., & Schmidt, W. H. *Models of the school improvement process: Factors contributing to success.* Andover, MA: NETWORK, 1982.

Dachler, H. P., & Wilpert, B. Conceptual dimensions and boundaries of participation in organizations: A critical evaluation. *Administrative Science Quarterly*, 1978, *23*, 1–39.

Dawson, J. A. Teacher participation in educational innovation: Some insights into its nature. Paper presented at the Annual Meeting of the American Educational Research Association, San Francisco, 1979.

Dawson J. A. Qualitative research findings: What do we do to improve and estimate their validity? Paper presented at the annual meeting of the American Educational Research Association, New York, 1982.

Deal, T. E., & Celotti, L. D. How much influence do (and can) educational administrators have on classrooms? *Phi Delta Kappan,* 1980, *60,* 471–73.

Deal, T. E., Meyer, J. W., & Scott, W. R. Organizational influences on educational technology. In J. V. Baldridge and T. E. Deal (Eds.), *Managing change in educational organizations: Sociological perspectives, strategies and case studies.* Berkeley, CA: McCutchan, 1975.

Deal, T. E., & Nutt, S. Promoting, guiding and surviving change in small school districts. Cambridge, MA: Abt Associates, 1979.

Devlin, B. S. Democratic leadership: Guidelines for school administrators. *Administrator's Notebook,* 1981, *29,* 1–4.

Emrick, J. A., Peterson, S. M., & Agarawala-Rogers, R. *Evaluation of the national diffusion network.* Menlo Park, CA: Stanford Research Institute, 1977.

English, F. W. *Quality control and curriculum development.* Arlington, VA: American Association of School Administrators, 1978.

Felker, R. M., & Davis, W. J. Change and participation: A review and critique of selected literature (Theoretical Paper No. 75). Madison, WI: Wisconsin Research and Development Center for Individualized Schooling, University of Wisconsin, 1979.

Firestone, W. A. Participation and influence in the planning of educational change. *Journal of Applied Behavioral Science,* 1977, *13*(2), 163–183.

Firestone, W. A. *Great expectations for small schools.* New York: Praeger, 1980.

Firestone, W. A., & Corbett, H. D. *Rationality and cooperation in external assistance for school improvement.* Philadelphia: Research for Better Schools, 1979.

Firestone, W. A., & Corbett, H. D. Schools versus linking agents as contributors to the change process. *Educational Evaluation and Policy Analysis,* 1981, *3*(2), 5–17.

Firestone, W. A., & Herriott, R. *Images of schools as organizations: An exploration of their conceptualization, measurement, and correlates.* Philadelphia: Research for Better Schools, 1981. (a)

Firestone, W. A., & Herriott, R. Images of the organization and the promotion of change. In R. Corwin (Ed.), *Research in sociology of education and socialization: Vol. 2. Research on educational organizations.* Greenwich, CT: JAI Press, 1981. (b)

Firestone, W. A., & Herriott, R. Two images of schools as organizations: An explication and illustrative empirical test. *Educational Administration Quarterly,* 1982, *18*(2), 39–59.

Fullan, M. School district and school personnel in knowledge utilization. In R. Lehming and M. Kane (Eds.), *Improving schools: Using what we know*. Beverly Hills, CA: Sage, 1981.

Fullan, M. *The meaning of educational change*. New York: Teachers College Press, 1982.

Fullan, M., & Pomfret, A. Research on curriculum and instruction implementation. *Review of Educational Research,* 1977, *47*(1), 335–397.

Giacquinta, J. B. The process of organizational change in schools. In F. N. Kerlinger (Ed.), *Review of research in education* (Vol. 1). Itasca, Ill.: F. E. Peacock Publishers, 1973.

Glaser, B. G., & Strauss, A. L. *The discovery of grounded theory: Strategies for qualitative research*. Chicago: Aldine, 1967.

Glaser, E. Durability of innovations in human service organizations. *Knowledge: Creation, Diffusion, Utilization,* 1981, *3*(2), 167–185.

Glatthorn, A. A. Curriculim change in loosely coupled systems. *Educational Leadership,* 1981, *39*(2), 110–113.

Greene, D., & David, J. L. *A research design for generalizing from multiple case studies*. Palo Alto: Bay Area Research Group, 1981.

Greenwood, P. W., Mann, D., & McLaughlin, M. *Federal programs supporting educational change: Vol. 3. The process of change*. Santa Monica, CA: Rand, 1975.

Gross, N., Giacquinta, J., & Bernstein, M. *Implementing organizational innovations: A sociological analysis of planned educational change*. New York: Basic Books, 1971.

Hage, J., & Aiken, M. *Social change in complex organizations*. New York: Random House, 1970.

Hall, G., & Loucks, S. F. A developmental model for determining whether the treatment is actually implemented. *American Educational Research Journal,* 1977, *14*(3), 263–276.

Hall, G., Zigarmi, P., & Hord, S. A taxonomy of interventions: The prototype and initial testing. Paper presented at the annual meeting of the American Educational Research Association, San Francisco, 1979.

Havelock, R. *The change agent's guide to innovation in education*. Englewood Cliffs, NJ: Educational Technology Publications, 1973.

Herriott, R. E., & Gross, N. (Eds.). *The dynamics of planned educational change: Case studies and analyses*. Berkeley, CA: McCutchan, 1979.

Hood, P. D., & Blackwell, L. Key educational information users and their styles of information use. In *The educational information market study* (Vol. 1). San Francisco: Far West Laboratory for Educational Research and Development, 1976.

Huberman, A. M., & Miles, M. B. Drawing valid meaning from qualitative data: Some techniques of data reduction and display. Paper presented at the annual meeting of the American Educational Research Association, New York, 1982.

Katz, D., & Kahn, R. L. *The social psychology of organizations.* New York: Wiley, 1966.

Kirst, M. W., & Walker, D. F. An analysis of curriculum policy-making. *Review of Educational Research,* 1971, *41,* 479–509.

Kozuch, J. A. Implementing an educational innovation: The constraints of the school setting. *High School Journal,* 1979, *62*(5), 223–231.

Larsen, J., & Werner, P. Measuring utilization of mental health program consultation. In J. Ciarlo (Ed.), *Utilization evaluation: Concepts and measurements techniques.* Beverly Hills, CA: Sage, 1981.

Lecompte, M. D., & Goetz, J. P. Problems of reliability and validity in ethnographic research. *Review of Educational Research,* 1982, *52*(1), 31–60.

Lindblom, C., & Cohen, D. *Usable knowledge.* New Haven, CT: Yale University Press, 1979.

Lortie, D. C. The balance of control and autonomy in elementary school teaching. In A. Etzioni (Ed.), *The semi-professions and their organizations.* New York: Free Press, 1969.

Lortie, D. C. *Schoolteacher.* Chicago: University of Chicago Press, 1975.

Loucks, S. F. People, practices, and policies: Discoveries from school improvement research. Paper presented at the joint annual meeting of the Pennsylvania and New Jersey Educational Research Associations, Philadelphia, 1982.

Louis, K. S. Dissemination of information from centralized bureaucracies to local schools: The role of the linking agent. *Human Relations,* 1977, *30*(1), 25–42.

Louis, K. S. External agents and knowlege utilization: Dimensions for analysis and action. In R. Lehming and M. Kane (Eds.), *Improving schools: Using what we know.* Beverly Hills, CA: Sage, 1981.

Louis, K. S., & Kell, D. *The human factor in knowledge use: Field agent roles in education.* Cambridge, MA: Abt Associates, 1981.

Louis, K. S., Rosenblum, S., & Molitor, J. *Linking R & D outcomes with local schools: Vol. 2. The process and outcomes of knowledge utilization.* Cambridge, MA: Abt Associates, 1981.

Mann, D. *Making change happen.* New York: Teachers College Press, 1978.

March, J. G., & Simon, H. A. *Organizations.* New York: Wiley, 1958.

McLaughlin, M. Implementation of ESEA Title I: A problem of compliance. *Teachers College Record,* 1976, *77*(3), 397–415.

McLaughlin, M., & Marsh, D. Staff development and school change. *Teachers College Record,* 1978, *80*(1), 69–94.

Miles, M. B. On temporary systems. In M. B. Miles (Ed.), *Innovation in education.* New York: Teachers College Press, 1964.

Miles, M. B. Qualitative data as an attractive nuisance: The problem of analysis. *Administrative Science Quarterly,* 1979, *24,* 590–601.

Miles, M. B. Mapping the common properties òf schools. In R. Lehming and M. Kane (Eds.), *Improving schools: Using what we know.* Beverly Hills, CA: Sage, 1981.

Miles, M. B. Innovation up close: A field study in 12 school settings. Paper presented at the School Improvement Seminar, U.S. Department of Education, Washington, D.C., 1982.

Paul, D. A. Change processes at the elementary, secondary, and postsecondary levels of education. In N. Nash and J. Culbertson (Eds.), *Linking processes in educational improvement: Concepts and applications.* Columbus, OH: University Council for Educational Administration, 1977.

Piele, P. *Review and analysis of the role, activities, and training of educational linking agents.* Eugene, OR: University of Oregon, ERIC Clearinghouse on Educational Management, 1975.

Rist, R. C. Blitzkrieg ethnography: On the transformation of a method into a movement. *Educational Researcher,* 1980, *9*(2), 8–10.

Rogers, E. *Diffusion of innovations.* New York: Macmillan, 1962.

Rosenblum, S., & Louis, K. S. *Stability and change.* New York: Plenum, 1981.

Ryan, B., & Gross, N. C. The diffusion of hybrid seed corn in two Iowa communities. *Rural Sociology,* 1943, *8,* 15–24.

Schuetz, A. Common-sense and scientific interpretation of human action. *Philosophy and Phenomenological Research,* 1953, *14,* 1–37.

Sieber, S. Knowledge utilization in public education: Incentives and discentives. In R. Lehming and M. Kane (Eds.), *Improving schools: Using what we know.* Beverly Hills, CA: Sage, 1981.

Smith, B. O., Stanley, W. O., & Shores, J. H. *Fundamentals of curriculum development* (Rev. ed.). New York: World Book, 1957.

Stearns, M. S., & Norwood, C. R. *Evaluation of the field test of project information packages.* Menlo Park, CA: Stanford Research Institute, 1977.

Taba, H. *Curriculum development: Theory and practice.* New York: Harcourt, Brace & World, 1962.

Thompson, J. D. *Organizations in action: Social science bases of administrative theory.* New York: McGraw-Hill, 1967.

Tyler, R. W. *Basic principles of curriculum and instruction.* Chicago: University of Chicago Press, 1949.

Waller, W. *The sociology of teaching* (3rd printing). New York: Wiley, 1967.

Weick, K. E. Educational organizations as loosely coupled systems. *Administrative Science Quarterly,* 1976, *21,* 1–19.

Weick, K. E. Administering education in loosely coupled schools. *Phi Delta Kappan,* 1982, *63*(10), 673–676.

Wilson, B. L., & Corbett, H. D. Organization and change: The effects of school linkages on the quantity of implementation. *Educational Administration Quarterly,* 1983, *19*(4), 85–104.

Wilson, S. The use of ethnographic techniques in educational research. *Review of Educational Research,* 1977, *47*(1), 245–265.

Yin, R. The case study as a serious research strategy. *Knowledge: Creation, Diffusion, Utilization,* 1981, *3*(1), 97–114.

Yin, R., Quick, S., Bateman, P., & Marks, G. *Changing urban bureaucracies: How new practices become routinized, executive summary.* Santa Monica, CA: Rand, 1978.

Zaltman, G., Florio, D., & Sikorski, L. *Dynamic educational change.* New York: Macmillan, 1977.

Index

Administrators: effects of, on project continuation, 116, 117; effects of, on project implementation, 106, 143–44; and field agent activities, 35; incentives for, 123–24; and meeting arrangements, 26–27; and project leadership, 40, 42–43, 110; as source of incentives, 120, 121–24, 130, 152, 155, 157, 158, 162, 168, 170; and staff tensions, 37–38, 150, 154; turnover of, 38–39

Basic skills, 15–16, 47, 55–58, 68–71, 140–41
Berman, Paul, 7, 8, 10, 64, 65–66, 113–114, 115, 126, 142
Bigtown Senior High School, 17, 22, 34, 49, 69, 75, 94, 99, 118, 165–67; commitment to change in, 88; curriculum in, 107; district's relationship with, 123; field agent's role in, 30–31; incentives in, 80–82, 121, 123; participation in, 85–86; planning team in, 40, 84–85; resource availability in, 36, 53; state requirements for, 82

Career education, 16, 47, 56–59, 67–71
Citizen education, 16–17, 47, 57–58, 60–61, 67–71
Change outcomes, 11–12. *See also* Continuation; Implementation
Clerical support. *See* Resources
Continuation, 12–13, 112–33, 144–45; appropriate unit of analysis for,

116–17, 125; and curriculum, 126–29; definition of, 4, 113–14; and effectiveness assessments, 129–30; extent of, 116, 117–18; and incentives, 119–26; and postimplementation events, 114–15, 117; prospects for, 112
Current practices, 7–8, 139–40, 188; as decision making, 139–40; as ordinary knowledge, 55–57, 140; and planning, 54–57, 62; and use of planning periods, 110
Curriculum: and continuation, 117–18, 126–29, 131, 145; decisions about, 106–7; development of, 9; enforcement of, 94–95; and staff turnover, 128; and state requirements, 128; and teacher behavior, 108, 126–28, 163–64. *See also* Linkages, in subunits

Decision making. *See* Current practices
Disincentives. *See* Incentives

Effectiveness assessments, 129–30, 131; by administrators, 130; and continuation, 119, 129–30, 145; by teachers, 129–30
Expertise. *See* Resources

Factions, 7, 138–39, 150, 154, 161, 186–87; and field agents, 37–38; and participation, 89; and planning, 59–60, 63

203